IT'S YOUR LIFE ENJOY IT!

Carlton Myers

BROADMAN PRESS
NASHVILLE, TENNESSEE

© Copyright 1990 ● Broadman Press
All rights reserved
4250-90
ISBN: 0-8054-5090-4
Dewey Decimal Classification: 248.4
Subject Heading: CHRISTIAN LIFE
Library of Congress Catalog Card Number: 89-27076
Printed in the United States of America

Library of Congress Cataloging-in-Publication Data

Myers, Carlton L., 1920-
    It's your life—enjoy it! / Carlton L. Myers.
        p. cm.
    ISBN 0-8054-5090-4
    1. Christian life--Baptist authors. I. Title.
BV4501.2.M89 1990
248.4'861—dc20

89-27076
CIP

*To my wife Vera
and my sons Paul and David*

Contents

1
We Are Meant for Joy

The Abundant Life

God intends for everyone to enjoy life to the fullest. Regardless of the circumstances of a person's life, he or she can experience the abundant life. This life is not dependent on health, financial standing, social position, or external stimuli. It is a life in tune with heaven and eternity—"geared to the times but anchored to the rock."

One prayer of the church calls this life a "valley of tears." This prayer does not express the teachings of the Bible in the Gospels or the Epistles. Life is *not* a bowl of cherries covered with vinegar.

This book will show how one can enjoy life to the fullest and live it within the boundaries of the biblical ethic. "The chief end of man is to glorify God and to *enjoy* Him forever," states the *Westminster Confession*. Listen to Jesus:

> I am come that they might have life, and that they might have it more abundantly (John 10:10).

> I have come in order that you might have life—life in all its fullness (John 10:10, GNB).

> I have come that they may have life, and have it to the full (John 10:10, NIV).

My purpose is to give life in all its fullness (John 10:10, TLB).

The preceding four versions of John 10:10 show that Jesus intended His people to enjoy the abundant life. The *abundant life* means one that includes a lot of genuine joy.

The Bible on the Subject of Joy

Not only did Jesus emphasize that He came to give us abundant life—life to its fullest—but the Bible is full of joy even as the ocean is full of salt water.

The Bible contains about 150 references to some form of the word *joy*. At least one third of them are in the New Testament. This does not count the hundreds of times the word *rejoice* appears in both testaments. For example, the apostle Paul wrote to the church at Rome, "Now the God of hope fill you with all joy and peace in believing, that ye may abound in hope, through the power of the Holy Ghost" (Rom. 15:13).

Paul also spoke of joy as being the result of the Holy Spirit working in our lives: "But the fruit of the Spirit is love, *joy*, peace, long-suffering, gentleness" (Gal. 5:22, author's italics).

Others in the Bible also dealt with joy. The apostle John wrote the following words: "These things write we unto you, that your joy may be full" (1 John 1:4).

According to God's written Word, the Lord intends for the Christian life to be packed with and overflowing with joy. Jesus came to give us eternal life which in turn supplies abundant life. What does the word *joy* mean?

Webster's dictionary tells us that *joy* is the emotion evoked by well-being, success, or good fortune—or by the prospect of possessing what one desires. It is a state of inward elation and a sense of well-being.

The Difference Between Happiness and Joy

The distinction between *happiness* and *joy* is in accord with life's experiences. What is this difference? *Happiness* depends upon the happenings, the circumstances, the events, and the occurrences in a person's life. However, *joy* depends upon the relationship to and the fellowship with the Heavenly Father. Joy, as noted earlier and as stated in Galatians 5:22, is a fruit of the Holy Spirit, regardless of the circumstances of our lives. Therefore, it is possible to be joyful without being happy. It is possible to be joyful regardless of what happens in a person's life.

Although the Declaration of Independence declares that people have the right to the pursuit of happiness, it does not guarantee us happiness, only the right to pursue it.

Joy in Times of Suffering

Though a person cannot always be happy, joy can be his in spite of it all. Christians have the right to joy and the abundant life. The trials of life can, and often do, snatch happiness away from people, but they never need to rob them of the joy that comes from the Holy Spirit.

Some of the trials that can destroy a person's happiness—but not his inner joy if the Holy Spirit is allowed to produce joy in his life—are:

Death of a loved one.
Serious accident.
Senility of an elderly parent.
Desertion of a wife or husband.

Old age.
Serious surgical procedure.
Frustration of rearing teenagers.
Heart attack.
Cancer.
Mental illness of a relative or friend.
Loneliness.
Loss of home.
Terminal illness.
Unemployment.
Impaired sight or hearing.

The Results of Joy

What are the results of joy, even in devastating circumstances? Joy does not always result in a beaming, smiling face. It is possible to have joy within, even though it is not showing in a person's facial expression.

It is difficult to laugh or smile when your heart is breaking. However, it is possible to have inner peace and joy even then. How is this possible? The apostle Paul answered this question by saying, "We know that all things work together for good to them that love God, to them who are the called according to his purpose" (Rom. 8:28). Paul did not say that all things are good, but that all things work together for good—even in dreadful circumstances of a person's life.

The effects of joy result in physical, mental, emotional, and spiritual health. Joy leads to a thankful heart in the midst of trials, peace, and serenity.

Returning from Germany after World War II, I was sailing in the hold of a troop ship. A violent storm shook the vessel, and the ship pitched up and down violently. The other soldiers and I were frightened. Suddenly, the ship seemed to rise higher than before and plunged down into the ocean. We feared the worst. Almost at once, driven by panic, all of us stormed for the deck. Even as we did, the calm voice of the captain came over the loudspeaker: "Now hear this. Now hear this. Every soldier is ordered to return to his bunk immediately." The command was repeated several times.

Having been trained to obey orders, we returned to our bunks, cringing with fear and apprehension. We found out later that the ship was in no danger, nor were we. Gradually, the fear and anxiety vanished, and peace was restored in their place.

Sometimes calamity strikes us, and we may think the joy of the Lord has taken a sabbatical.

What good would the joy of the Lord be if it flowed into people's lives only when all was peaceful, calm, and successful? Our Lord meant for His joy to reign in good times and bad. This thought almost reminds me of wedding vows—"in sickness and in health, in poverty and wealth."

2
The Source of Joy

What Will Not Bring Joy into Your Life

The late J. Paul Getty, at one time the richest man in the world, wrote of his unhappiness in his memoirs. He lamented that he had gone through five marriages and had never "married well." Like many rich tycoons before and since, he testified that money could not buy him happiness. Neither poverty nor wealth determine our capacity for joy. If money could make a person happy, what amount would be required?

Countless uninformed people believe the Bible teaches that "money is the root of all evil." That is not the case. Rather, the apostle Paul observed, "The love of money is a root of all kinds of evil" (1 Tim. 6:10, NIV).

Of course, money can do plenty for us in our kind of society. One wag commented, "Money can't buy happiness, but it sure can help you select the kind of misery you enjoy. It can pay the mortgage on a house, care for the monthly payments on a car, handle the necessities of life, and even buy a few luxuries. Money can also meet the expenses of the church and send missionaries to the far corners of the earth. One thing that money cannot do is guarantee happiness, and it can never bring true joy into your life.

Power Will Not Bring Joy

Throughout history, certain movements have chanted "power to the people." All too often, only certain people have had power. One statesman mused that "power corrupts, and absolute power corrupts absolutely." Power can be used for evil. In the wrong hands it can be wielded to manipulate persons for personal gain, whether financially, politically, or otherwise. Despots, big and little, have wreaked havoc in society, in institutions, and even in religious organizations.

On the other hand, though, power can be employed for righteous, worthy ends. Military power defeated the forces of the Axis powers in World War II. Police power can apprehend and punish criminals. Power of the press can expose evil that crooked persons have tried to conceal. *Human* power will not usher joy into a life, but the power of God's Holy Spirit will (see Acts 1:8).

Popularity and Fame Will Not Bring Joy

President Johnson had a landslide victory in his bid for the presidency. His popularity was enormous. After a few years, he decided not to run for reelection because he felt his popularity had eroded and almost vanished. His advisors sensed that he might lose a bid for reelection.

President Nixon had an overwhelming victory for reelection. Pollsters called him at the time one of the most popular presidents in history. Later, he resigned in disgrace as his popularity evaporated in the wake of the Watergate scandal.

Popularity is fleeting and transient. Public entertainers and sports figures argue that they want to make all they can while they can because popularity is brief. A person who is a hero today can become the "goat" in a short while. The more popularity one has in life, the more he stands to lose.

Popularity cannot guarantee happiness and joy in anybody's life.

What Will Bring Joy?

Joy is the result of a right relationship with God, fellowship with our Lord and Savior Jesus Christ and our Christian brothers and sisters, and the Holy Spirit working in and through people.

Right Relationship with God.

The Bible reveals to us that a right relationship with God begins with a genuine conversion experience. It is sometimes referred to as being "born again," "regeneration," "the new birth," or "salvation." This conversion experience is the result of three following decisions.

● *Acceptance* of Jesus Christ as your Lord and Savior. Jesus died in place of sinful persons as their substitute. (Refer to John 1:12.)

● *Belief* that Jesus died for your sins. (Refer to Acts 16:31.)

● *Commitment* to a biblical, Christian life-style which involves living for God's glory and doing His will. (Refer to Luke 9:23.)

Fellowship with Jesus and Other Christians.

When a husband and wife quarrel, they are still married, but their fellowship may be temporarily broken. The joy of the marriage momentarily wanes, but it returns as soon as they are reconciled, usually by one or both saying something like, "I'm sorry. I was wrong. Please forgive me."

If the joy has gone out of a person's life, perhaps he or she needs to "make up" with the Lord by confessing, "I'm sorry, Lord. I was wrong. Please forgive me."

The Holy Spirit Working in and Through Us.

A classic Scripture verse teaches people that joy is a result of the Holy Spirit's working in and through us. The verse is: "The fruit of the Spirit is love, joy, peace, long-suffering, gentleness, goodness, faith, meekness, temperance" (Gal. 5:22-23). The Holy Spirit activates and energizes the person who has a right relationship with God and is in fellowship with Jesus and other Christians, producing "joy unspeakable and full of glory."

Joy Is the Result of a Biblical Life-style

What is a biblical life-style? It is living one's life according to the teachings of the Bible, of course. Genuine Christians can enjoy life to its fullest, even though many may not. Those outside of Christ often seem to be happy, but they will never know the joy of the Lord unless they receive Him. They may seem to be "really living," but they are fooling themselves. What happiness they have is temporary. To receive the most out of life, one must develop a biblical life-style.

A biblical life-style implies living according to the high moral and ethical standards of the Bible. It helps to be regular in your attendance at church and Bible study, to attend other Bible classes and study programs, listen to the preaching and teaching of the Word of God, and have your own devotion time with prayer and intensive Bible reading.

A Formula for Joy

The *Westminster Confession* presents a formula for joy in these words: "The chief end of man is to glorify God and to enjoy Him forever." Write this formula indelibly in your mind and heart. It is the secret for true and lasting joy. The psalmist expressed it well as he prayed to God, "In thy presence is fullness of joy: at they right hand there are pleasures for evermore" (Ps. 16:11).

This formula for the enjoyment of life is confirmed in both the Old and New Testaments. Note these verses:

"I have created him for my glory" (Isa. 43:7).

"Whether therefore ye eat, or drink, or whatsoever ye do, do all to the glory of God" (1 Cor. 10:31).

"For ye are bought with a price; therefore glorify God in your body, and in your spirit, which are God's" (1 Cor. 6:20).

Too many people have the mistaken idea that Christianity takes all the joy out of life, but the Bible teaches living for the glory of God puts joy into life.

Each person is to glorify God. By following the biblical life-style mentioned earlier, allowing the Holy Spirit to make people what God wants them to be, and doing what God wants them to do, God can be glorified.

3
Creating a Philosophy
of Life

The Need for a Philosophy of Life

Chapters 1 and 2 are similar to one's deciding to build a house. A house must have a foundation upon which to build. When the foundation is laid, one can then build the superstructure. The walls and the roof can be erected. This chapter corresponds to the walls and the roof. Later chapters will correspond to the inside part of the house. Consider creating a philosophy of life.

To enjoy life to its fullest, one begins with the acceptance of the fact that the chief end of mankind is to glorify God and enjoy Him forever. With this statement as the cornerstone of a person's life, he or she can construct the walls of his or her life—a philosophy of life.

Webster's dictionary says that philosophy is the pursuit of wisdom, a search for truth through logical reasoning rather than factual observation, and an analysis of the grounds of and concepts expressing fundamental beliefs. A philosophy of life defines the meaning and purpose of life. It is the basis of why and how people live.

Brief History of Philosophy

The history of philosophy has changed over the centuries. One could begin with the philosophy of Plato and Aristotle, who lived long before Christ. Or one could start with that system of philosophy known as idealism, continue to the system called naturalism, and continue through the centuries to logical empiricism or determinism until one comes to the confusing ideas of contemporary philosophy.

The preceding paragraph was given without explanation of the terminology or the systems merely to make the point that philosophical systems come and go, as do theological ones.

A student sat for months through classes in philosophy. Confused by the competing systems, he asked his professor, "Sir, what is *your* philosophy of life?"

The professor's answer was, "Young man, I have none."

What a tragedy that a college professor could know philosophy well enough to teach it but not have a philosophy of life of his own.

This book, without teaching a course in philosophy, will suggest a philosophy of life. However, in the end, one must create his own. And, even if a person never writes it on paper, he has created one in his mind. A person lives by his philosophy of life whether he realizes it or not. To enjoy life to the fullest, one needs to have a philosophy of life based on the formula that was stated earlier.

What Is a Philosophy of Life?

A philosophy of life is what guidelines a person chooses to live by. It's the meaning and purpose of life for him. It is based on his assumptions about life and includes a system of values and priorities. It gives direction to life.

The Bible does not present a formal philosophy of life set forth in propositional form. Neither does it present a formal, systematic theological system (formal doctrines, beliefs). The Bible does give people the basics for both and must be applied to their lives. A philosophy of life enables people to set their objectives, goals, and the direction of their lives. People are not like the mythical horse that ran in all directions.

A philosophy of life offers guidelines as to a person's beliefs and practices, morals, and decisions. Of course, the Christian needs the help of the Lord in creating his philosophy of life.

Must a person write out his philosophy of life? No, it is not an absolute necessity, but it definitely helps. A person can drive his car in an area that he is not familiar with and not use a map, but a map is a distinct asset. A person can receive oral directions from another, but he can't replace having a map to see the whole picture at one time.

As a map helps people determine which roads to take to arrive at their destination, so an individual philosophy of life helps persons to determine where they want to go and how they will make it. To write on paper a philosophy of life forces a person to do some thinking about the direction of her/his life, about what she believes, and what she will do in the future. To write a philosophy of life is a step in the direction of enjoying life to the fullest.

What Should a Philosophy of Life Include?

A philosophy of life should include a summary of basic beliefs about life, based on the Bible. It helps to write these beliefs on paper. This philosophy should note the purpose, objectives, and goals of one's life. Frequent evaluations should be made of this philosophy for possible changes as a person better understands what God wants him to do with his life. This philosophy should be followed by a strategy which will be discussed in chapter 4. It may take weeks, months, or even years to create, construct, or formulate a philosophy of life.

An Example of a Philosophy of Life

God's plan for each individual Christian is different. It is up to each person to discover God's plan for his life. A philosophy of life will help one to discover His plan.

What follows are the main parts of my philosophy of life. Note places where one agrees or disagrees. Decide how another philosophy of life ought to read in comparison to mine.

Article I: Definition of Philosophy

The original meaning of the word *philosophy* is derived from two Greek words which together mean "love of wisdom." Webster's dictionary defines philosophy as the science which investigates the facts and principles of reality and of human nature and conduct. Warren C. Young, said, "Philosophy is the attempt to provide an integrated world-view."[1]

Article II: Systems of Philosophy

The system which is close to mine is the "Christian

Realism" of Warren C. Young.

Article III: Christian Realism

A. Special Revelation. God has made Himself known by special revelation through the Written Word (Bible) and the Living Word (Jesus Christ).

B. Experience. The Christian life begins with a genuine conversion experience that affects the whole person(ality). Feeling, intellect, and will are involved. This experience involves a person's total commitment to Jesus Christ as Lord and Savior. This precludes any form of existentialism.

C. Faith and Reason. Faith without reason tends to fanaticism. Reason without faith tends to rationalism. Christian realism involves both faith and reason. The assurance and confirmation of one's conversion experience comes through the witness of the Holy Spirit and a changed life.

D. Christian Theism. Christian theism accepts the existence of the God of the Bible—His Trinity, that He is a personal and self-revealing God; that He is sovereign, omniscient, omnipotent, omnipresent; and that He is both a God of wrath and justice (to the unrepentant) and a God of mercy, grace, and love (to the unrepentant). He is absolute, without any limitation (except that which is self-imposed), and supreme in the universe. He is both transcendent and immanent. He exists, one God, as Father (Father of all humankind in a creating sense and Father of all Christians in a spiritual sense), Son (as described in the Apostles' Creed, Nicene Creed, Athanasian Creed, and *The Baptist Faith and Message*), and Holy Spirit (the Spirit being Deity and having personality).

E. Creation. "All things were created by God and are ever dependent on Him."[2] I reject all forms of evolution and accept progressive-creationism, as described by Bernard Ramm in *The Christian View of Science and Scripture*.

F. Human Beings. "Man is a rational and moral being, a complete spiritual personality."[3] Human beings are made in the image of God and are responsible for their choices. Each exists as one person, but with a dual nature, that is body, soul and spirit.

G. Evil. Two kinds of evil exist in the world. There is *moral* evil, which arose in humanity's willful rebellion against God. There is *natural* evil, such as disease, pain, suffering, calamities, and so forth.

H. Restoration. Lost, fallen humans are redeemed through repentance and faith in the substitutionary death of Christ for them. This repentance involves both sorrow for sin (for offending God) and intention to refrain from sin in the future. This faith includes commitment to the will of God.

There are three tenses in salvation: (1) salvation from the *penalty of past* sins, (2) salvation from the *power* of *present* sins, and (3) salvation from the *presence of future* sin (in heaven). Christian realism believes in both the immortality of the person and the resurrection of the body.

I. Truth. Truth may be learned through many channels, including logic and semantics. Some truth may be learned through *immediate* criteria (instinct, feeling, senses, or intuition). Some may be learned through *social* criteria (custom, tradition, and universal agreement). Some may be learned through *philosophical* criteria (correspondence, pragmatism, and coherence). Ultimate truth comes through the special revelation of God in the Bible and in Jesus Christ.

J. Dualism. Christian realism is dualistic. It rejects monism and instrumentalism.

K. Creationism. Christian realism rejects emergent evolution, organic evolution, and theistic evolution. It believes in creationism. "No scientific evidence has ever been produced to demonstrate that any living forms have emerged from non-living substances."[4]

L. Values. Man "has no rights and privileges in himself but he has them only from the hand of his Creator, and on the conditions set forth by the Creator. MAN IS ALWAYS RESPONSBILE TO GOD. The evils of this present age root themselves in man's rebellion against the will of his Creator.... The true nature of ideals and the realization of true values must begin with a new birth."[5]

Value for Christian realists are simply the will of God for them. "Value . . . is theonomous [God-centered], rather than autonomous [man-centered]. The ultimate standard or ideal of value . . . holiness . . . to do according to God's will is the ideal of life itself. . . . The obligation of the Christian life is first of all to God himself. He is to recognize God as God, and so to give him his rightful place. He is to obey the divine commands to give to God the adoration and worship which is his due."[6]

The Christian life includes self-respect, self-development, self-realization, and self-affirmation, but mostly it includes self-denial. Christ's goal for humanity is perfection.

Article IV: Purpose

A. Philosophy of Life. Realizing that every thinking person must develop a philosophy of life, I have developed and written this document. I accept the preceding and subsequent paragraphs as my philosophy of life.

B. My Life. The purpose of my life is expressed in the words of the *Westminster Confession of Faith* which says that the chief end of man is to glorify God and to enjoy Him forever. That which glorifies God is doing His will at all times. This is the meaning and purpose of life.

Article V: Theology

I accept as my doctrinal beliefs the teachings of the whole Bible; the interpretation of Young's "Christian realism," the three great ecumenical creeds of the Christian church (Apostles', Nicene, and Athanasian); the *Westminster Confession*; and the May 1963 revision of *The Baptist Faith and Message*.

Article VI: Objectives

I believe that I can best glorify God by carrying out the following objectives: (1) be the best husband and father possible, (2) be the best minister possible, and (3) be an author of articles and books.

Article VII: Evaluation

Under the leadership of the Holy Spirit, one should occasionally evaluate his/her philosophy of life.

Article VIII: Amendments

Amendments may be made at anytime after sufficient prayer and meditation.

Article IX: Programs and Priorities

In accordance with Article VI, my life shall be spent as follows: (1) husband and father, (2) clergyman, and (3) author.

Article X: My Christian Experience

A. Born of the flesh on June 26, 1919, approximately at 3:30 p.m. in the general hospital at Wilkes-Barre, Pennsylvania.

B. Born of the *Spirit* on July 18, 1945, approximately at 9:30 p.m. in an evangelistic tent meeting in Lincoln, Lincolnshire, England.

C. I rededicated my life on November 22, 1985, approximately at 8:00 p.m. in my home.

Of course, a person probably will not understand some of the words in the above philosophy of life. That is not important. What is important is that one understands the idea of how to write his own philosophy of life.

Begin to write a philosophy of life. Remember to build it around the formula for enjoying life to its fullest. Think about glorifying God and enjoying Him now and in eternity.

Notes

1. Warren C. Young, *A Christian Approach to Philosophy* (Grand Rapids: Baker Book House, 1954), 22.
2. Young, 212.
3. Ibid.
4. Young, 103.
5. Ibid.
6. Ibid.

4
Strategy for Living

What Is a Strategy for Living?

The foundation, roof, and walls are to a building what philosophy of life is to a person. The inside of a house (such as the electrical and plumbing systems) is a part of the complete house, just as a strategy for living is a part of a person's life. Just as a person needs a philosophy of life (as a house needs a foundation, walls, and roof), one needs a strategy for living.

A strategy for living is based on one's philosophy of life; enables her to make the best use of her time, abilities, and spiritual gifts; and helps her to live life to the maximum.

Your Purpose for Living Is Its Basis

A strategy of living must be in complete agreement with one's philosophy of life, just as all the parts of a building must be properly constructed, and as electrical and plumbing systems must fit into the walls. The foundation of a house determines where the walls will be built. The walls determine where the roof and the electrical and plumbing systems will be put.

Setting Long-range Goals

Even the elderly should continue to set goals. Every person ought to have short-range and long-range goals. What does one want to accomplish during the rest of his life? The following list includes some examples of long-range goals:

To pay off one's home mortgage.

To make it to the Baseball Hall of Fame.

To become a widely known author.

To travel to the Holy Land, Switzerland, and Australia.

To make a million dollars in business in order to help worthy causes.

To lead at least one hundred people to Christ.

Be sure to make long-range goals (and all other goals) specific, measurable, and obtainable (with the help of the Lord). Do not set vague, general goals, such as to be Christian, a good parent, or a rich person. Prayerfully choose long-range goals that are in line with one's philosophy of life and what one believes is God's will for him.

Obviously, a person must consider members of her family as well as her own abilities, skills, talents, and gifts. Also one must be honest about her assets, liabilities, and limitations.

Setting Intermediate Goals

Since long-range goals are a person's ultimate goals, intermediate-range goals are a person's near-at-hand factors to consider. Intermediate goals are those that one plans to accomplish along with and via to his long-range goals. Since long-range goals may encompass thirty, forty, or fifty years in a person's future, intermediate-range goals will encompass a shorter span of years. Intermediate goals are what a person plans to accomplish in the next ten or twenty years. They must be reached before a person can reach his long-range goals.

Based on the examples of long-range goals previously mentioned, here are some examples of intermediate-range goals:

To be in good health when one reaches the age of forty.

To have half the home mortgage paid off in fifteen years.

To lead at least fifty people to Christ by the year 2000.

To continue to be happily married.

To publish either a nonfiction book or a novel.

To become a major league baseball player.

One can see that to achieve any of the long-range goals noted previously, a person will have to achieve his intermediate-range goals first.

Short-term or Immediate Goals

Long-range and intermediate-range goals may seem impossible to attain or so far off in the future as to discourage one from attaining them. So a person will need to determine some short-term or immediate goals for a short period of time (three to five years).

Using the same examples of long-range and interme-diate-range goals previously mentioned, the following list is a sample of short-range goals one will need to ac-complish. Remember to consider one's family, abilities, and philosophy of life.

To lose 15 pounds.

To purchase a house in the next five years.

To have two children in the next five years.
To have family worship in the home.
To go into the restaurant business.
To take a course in personal evangelism.
To work at being a good spouse.
To write a book.
To be a minor-league baseball player.

Setting Priorities

In line with one's goals, set certain priorities for the use of time, money, and energy. Here are some examples:

Find time to exercise for half an hour daily.

After taking out the tithe, the first budget item will be to pay on the home mortgage note.

Rearing children will take priority in one's life over occupation, profession, or job.

Have family worship daily after supper.

Find time to practice the piano one hour daily.

Study the restaurant business carefully.

Engage daily in life-style evangelism.

Give priority to being a loving spouse.

Find at least one hour a day to work on a book.

Practice pitching a baseball every weekday.

The following is an example of a strategy for living:

Strategy for Living
(how to make the best use of one's time and abilities)

I. Long-Range Goals

  A. Articles—Sell 75 percent of articles submitted.

    1. Mail one article per month.

    2. Send out one query per month.

    3. Do not write article until OK is received on query.

B. Nonfiction Books—Publish at least one book.
   1. Send formal book proposal.
   2. Research before writing early drafts.
   3. Mail several chapters.
   4. Mail complete book to publisher.
C. Novels—Publish at least one novel.
   1. Write first draft.
   2. Revise, revise, revise.
   3. Mail final draft to publisher.
II. Short-Term Goals
   A. Work in an interim pastorate.
   B. Perform supply preaching.
   C. Lose 15 pounds by October 1.
   D. Practice the organ and piano. Vocalize daily.
   E. Listen to classical records daily.

If you have completed the suggested exercises for this chapter, then Chapter 5 will hopefully mean even more to you.

5
Developing
Sound Stewardship—Time

Everyone has the same amount of time in the day. What each person does not know is how much time he or she has to live. In this respect, one knows as much about the length of his life as the wisest, wealthiest, or most powerful person in the world.

When a person is young, he feels as if his future stretches out endlessly; so, to waste time does not seem bad. One may think, what's a few years at this stage of life? When a person is retired, he realizes that his future years are numbered, and he really cannot afford to waste any time.

Use of Time Based on Philosophy and Strategy for Living

How one uses her time should be based on her philosophy of life, strategy for living, and purpose in life. Any time not spent in that direction is a squandering of time. Time is too valuable to waste at any stage of a person's life. Every moment should lead a person to the goals he has set.

Time can be wasted or invested. Lost time can never be regained. It is gone forever. It is useless to say, "If I had my life to live over again, I would . . ." The past is gone forever. A person cannot be sure of any future.

The only reality is the present.

The Bible on Time

Various Hebrew and Greek words for *time* appear hundreds of times in the Bible. Let us examine a few of the biblical references to the word *time*.

"My times are in thy hand" (Ps. 31:15). Since the Bible teaches that God is omnipotent (all-powerful) and omniscient (all-knowing) and that He is sovereign (king), one can rest in the knowledge that he is in His hands.

"Cast me not off in the time of old age; forsake me not when my strength faileth" (Ps. 71:9). Sometimes elderly people feel they are being shut off—out of sight, out of mind. But they are never forgotten by the God who has a perfect memory, and who cares for every living person, regardless of age, race, color, creed, sect, or social standing.

> To every thing there is a season, and a time to every purpose under the heaven:
>
> A time to be born, and a time to die; a time to plant, and a time to pluck up that which is planted.
>
> A time to kill, and a time to heal; a time to break down, and a time to build up.
>
> A time to weep, and a time to laugh; a time to mourn, and a time to dance;
>
> A time to cast away stones, and a time to gather stones together; a time to embrace, and a time to refrain from embracing;
>
> A time to get, and a time to lose; a time to keep, and a time to cast away;
>
> A time to rend, and a time to sew; a time to keep silence, and a time to speak;
>
> A time to love, and a time to hate; a time of war,

and a time of peace (Eccl. 3:1-8).

This Hebrew poem assures people that every human activity has its appropriate time. These times appear in cycles on a regular basis.

Turning to the New Testament, one finds an important verse that needs to be rightly understood if he is to enjoy life. The verses say, "Behold, now is the accepted time; behold, now is the day of salvation" (2 Cor. 6:2).

Left in its context (setting), this passage shows that the apostle Paul informed the church at Corinth that the time had arrived for the fulfillment of God's gracious promises. This is a probable reference to promises expressed in previous chapters of his epistle.

Scripture verses have: (1) a proper interpretation in the light of their context, including their historical settings and (2) a spiritual application for today's people, so long as that spiritual application is not contrary to a specific teaching of Scripture. Therefore, the verse mentioned earlier has many spiritual applications, and many ministers have preached on these. For instance, it can be rightly said that "now is the accepted time" for salvation, for one to get right with God, and for one to start obeying His laws. But *now* is not always the proper time for certain other actions.

It has been said that one should never put off until tomorrow what should be done today. The opposite is likewise true that one should never do today what should be done tomorrow. Timing is important! There is a proper time to do all things, and if a person is to enjoy life to the fullest, he or she must perform the right acts at the right times. In other words, *now* is the time to do what needs to be done now. *Now* is not the time to do what should be done at some other time. In this chapter, one can discover the right time to do what needs to be done.

Classic verses on the use of time are found in the apostle Paul's Letters to the Ephesians and the Colossians. "Redeeming the time, because the days are evil" (Eph. 5:16). "Walk in wisdom toward them that are without, redeeming the time" (Col. 4:5). These verses inform Christians that they should not waste time, but they should realize as Christian stewards that time is a precious and priceless commodity. Therefore, it should be redeemed (invested) in a manner that will glorify God, enable one to reach his goals, and result in the enjoyment of life.

Keeping Track of Time

If I were to ask a person what he does with his time, he would tell me how he thinks he spends it. If I were to ask a person how much time he wastes, he would probably give me an answer that would not accurately describe how he uses his time or how much time he wastes.

The only way to know for sure how you use your time is to keep an accurate record of your schedule for a period of time. If a person does this, he will probably be shocked. Record for one week (starting now) everything you do with your time. Be specific. List as many of your actual actions as possible while you are at work. This will require discipline. This exercise is necessary so you can know exactly how much time you spend on each activity.

A person may discover that he is spending six or seven hours an evening watching television. Is that wise stewardship of the precious gift of time? Will it help you to reach the goals you set in your strategy for living? Reread your philosophy of life and strategy for living and note the goals. Work out a tentative time schedule based on your goals. Of course, you will have to develop it in relation to your family, job, energy, health, and so forth.

Prioritize Schedule

Before you make a final schedule, consider prioritizing time into three categories. In fact, some people may need to do this at the beginning of each day.

A items are those activities that *must* be completed that day. They may be doctor's appointments, handling the mortgage payment, getting to work, washing the clothes, going to church, shopping at the supermarket, reading a daily devotion, and the like.

B items are those activities that *should* be completed today, but only after all the *A* items have been done. They are important items, but they could be postponed until another day if necessary. For example, visiting a neighbor might be done the next day.

C activities are those which a person wants to do sometime, when he has some free time and has no *A* or *B* items to be done that day. For example, making a card catalog of one's books, writing on one's autobiography, or painting the porch would be *C* activities. Look at the following example of a time schedule for a working man or woman.

Sunday
7:00 - Rise and shine. Take care of personal items.
7:15 - Read devotion.
7:30 - Eat breakfast.
7:45 - Finish personal items.
8:00 - Watch religious program on TV.

9:00 - Get dressed for church.
9:30 - Leave for Sunday School.
10:00 - Attend Sunday School.
11:00 - Attend the worship service.
12:30 - Prepare lunch.
1:30 - Eat lunch.
2:00 - Read the Sunday paper. Watch TV. Take a walk.
5:00 - Prepare supper.
5:30 - Eat supper.
6:00 - Watch the news on TV.
7:00 - Attend the evening church service.

Monday—Friday
6:45 - Rise and shine. Take care of personal items.
7:00 - Read devotion and exercise.
7:30 - Eat breakfast.
7:45 - Finish personal items.
8:00 - Leave for work.
8:30 - Work.
12:00 - Eat lunch.
12:30 - Work.
5:00 - Leave work.
5:30 - Eat supper.
6:00 - Watch the news on TV.
7:00 - Read and spend time with family.

Saturday
8:00 - Rise and shine. Take care of personal items.
8:15 - Read devotion and exercise.
8:30 - Eat breakfast.
9:00 - Clean house, wash laundry, mow the lawn, and go shopping.
12:00 - Eat lunch.
1:00 - Visit a friend, neighbor, and/or prospective

church member.
5:30 - Eat supper.
6:00 - Watch the news on TV.
7:00 - Go to a concert or recital, visit friends, or watch
TV.

Should a Time Schedule Be Rigid?

Since a person cannot know in advance what will happen at times, schedules must not be rigid. There will always be interruptions, unexpected events, unavoidable delays, telephone calls, unexpected visitors, emergencies, and so forth. These will cause a person to alter (temporarily) his time schedule. Do not feel guilty when this happens.

Time schedules are guidelines, not rigid rules for how a person will spend his time. They are well worth constructing and well worth following, as much as possible. However, time schedules must be subject to change as conditions change, as goals change, or as interruptions occur that one does not know about in advance or cannot prevent.

The apostle Paul emphasized that people should be "redeeming the time, because the days are evil" (Eph. 5:16). Time schedules help us to redeem and use time in order to reach a person's goals and glorify God.

6
Material Resources

In earlier chapters we have learned that God meant for us to enjoy life in spite of the circumstances. We have discussed planning, priorities, and strategies which may help us in living a full and meaningful life. Now we approach one of the most controversial areas of one's life—material resources.

Managing Financial Resources

In this chapter, one can learn how to enjoy life through the management of financial resources. Financial management should enable a person to reach his goals and not merely to get by, living from hand to mouth or existing from payday to payday. If people do not learn to manage their financial resources properly, they will undoubtedly not enjoy their lives, because they will be constantly worrying about their financial condition.

The management of financial resources is often called Christian stewardship by the church. Other parts of Christian stewardship have to do with how we spend our time, talents, and energy. Christian stewards are managers of their financial resources for God. This is the plan of God for all Christians. It is not an option. The word *steward* in the *King James Version* of the Bible is the Greek word *oikonomos,* which refers to a slave (servant) given the responsibility of the management of the property of his owner.

It is an axiom taught in the Bible that *all* a person has, including his financial resources, belongs to God, not simply a tithe. People are to manage their (God's) property. In other words, God is the owner of Christians and all they have. They are stewards or trustees of their (God's) property.

The Christian management of financial resources is more than just giving to church and charity. People are also responsible to God for how they spend every penny they earn, spend, and save. How people spend the 90 percent of what they do not give directly to the church is as important in the sight of God as how they spend the first 10 percent.

How people manage financial resources is a part of their life-style and is bound up in whether or not they enjoy life. Discipline in this area should help people enjoy life.

People are often referred to as the children of God. In some cases, perhaps they should be called the "adults of God." Certainly, in the area of money management, people should grow up to be mature Christian stewards. Poor management of financial resources can take the joy out of life in a hurry. Proper money management is a source of joy, regardless of how much money and other material goods a person may possess. To enjoy life, plan to manage financial resources. Without a plan, one spends his money on a day-to-day, "play-it-by-ear" basis which can lead to financial chaos and ruin.

A Plan for Managing Financial Resources

The following steps build a plan by which a person can exercise his Christian stewardship concerning his financial resources.

Step 1: Establish Goals

Having already established long-term, intermediate-term, and short-term goals for one's life, now one needs to set up the same kind of goals for the management of money. These goals should enable a person to reach the life goals set up in Chapter 4.

First, write long-term financial goals. Prioritize these goals. Then write financial goals for the next five or ten years and financial goals for the next two years.

Step 2: Determine Income

Before a person can determine how to spend his money, he ought to know what his income will be. For those whose income varies considerably, an estimated income will do. List weekly, monthly, and annual income. This should include salary, interest on investments, Social Security benefits, receipts from pensions, and so forth. If a person borrows money for a home, car, or other need, list the loan as income.

Write the correct totals in the following list.

Gross Annual Income . . . . $
    Less Social Security taxes . . . . $
    Less other payroll deductions . . . . $
Net Annual Income . . . . $
    Amount borrowed . . . . $
    Other income . . . . $
Total Annual Net Income . . . . $
Total Monthly Net Income . . . . $

Step 3: Determine Last Year's Expenditures

If a person has kept a record of the major expenses that she incurred in the previous year, she can easily begin to determine her expenses for this year and future years.

List the following two types of expenses that were incurred last year.

A. Fixed expenses. These are costs of such things as mortgage payments (or rent), car payments, and insurance.

B. Variable expenses. These expenses are things such as food, clothing, utilities, and recreation.

A person can live without a budget, but without such a plan for managing money she will probably spend more than she should on many items and buy a lot due to impulse. A budget is not a tool to take the joy out of life. It is a management plan to put the joy into life. A budget is not a straitjacket but a guideline to help a person determine his income and expenditures. To follow a budget takes discipline and, believe it or not, with discipline comes joy.

Step 4: Prepare a Budget

If a person is single, he or she determines his or her own budget. If persons are married, they should prepare a budget together. If people have families, why not involve the children in this process? Use their input, evaluating it in light of their ages and maturity. This helps them gain practical experience for their lives when they become adults. A person might be able to prepare a budget in an hour. It may take many hours, days, or longer. It is too important to do it hurriedly. Take whatever time is necessary to do a good job of it.

Remember that a time schedule is flexible, and a budget should be the same. Use the following suggestions when preparing a budget.

1. *Make the Budget Flexible.* No one will ever be able to determine in advance every single expense item. Medical emergencies, automobile breakdowns, and the like will cause one's budget to vary. Keep that in mind and prepare for these situations by having some money set aside for contingencies.

    Enjoying life is not "keeping up with the Joneses." It is managing money in accordance with life goals, financial goals, and Christian stewardship obligations. A person has not failed if he finds that he cannot live completely on his budget or if he has to revise it from time to time. Adjust to changing circumstances. Everyone encounters unexpected expenses. Allow for some emergencies when budgeting, if possible.

2. *Make the Budget for the Family.* A person can find in books and pamphlets sample budgets for average families. However, there probably are no "average" families. Each family is different from every other family.

    How much you spend on each item depends on the size of the family, life-style, standard of living, health, education, resources, responsibilities, and tastes.

3. *Write the Budget on Paper.* Unless someone has a perfect memory, he will want to put in writing his plan of expenditures. Then every member of the family can see what the money management plan is.

4. *Provide for Unpaid Bills.* If a person has unpaid

bills, credit charges, or other debts, then the money owed belongs to somebody else.

In your budget provide for all your monthly bills, especially those fixed expenses over which you have little or no control. If you borrow to pay past due bills, be sure not to end up with a much larger debt than you already have.

5. *Plan for the Future.* If one's budget calls for the disbursement of all of one's income each pay period (as it does for many) and has no plan for savings for the future, a person could be in trouble.

In planning for the future, everyone should consider the following items:

• *Insurance.* Consider an all-around insurance plan that covers life, health, accident, fire, property, and liability.

• *Savings.* Many financial advisers recommend an emergency fund in the bank that will cover a person for three to six months at least. This is for emergencies not covered by one's budget. Put savings where they will earn the largest amount of interest. Ask a financial planner about certificates of deposit and IRA's. Even though these are not really meant for emergencies, they are good ways to save for the future.

• *Investments.* There are some definite rules concerning the investment of money in stocks, bonds, real estate, or other investments. They are (1) don't invest money that is needed to pay for fixed expenses or food, clothing, and shelter; (2) don't use savings that are kept for emergencies and investment purposes; and (3) investment money should be money one can afford to lose, if that should happen.

● *Retirement.* One may say, "I don't have to worry about retirement. I've got Social Security." But, if Social Security monthly payments are all a person has to live on when he retires, he will probably be living then on a considerably lower standard of living than he is now. A person will need more income than what he will get from Social Security. Do not depend on Social Security for financial survival when one retires.

If a person is planning on Medicare and/or Medicaid to pay all her medical expenses when she retires, she will discover too late that those programs will not. An IRA or a private medical-surgical plan is needed. Start those now.

● *Estate Planning.* People can't take it with them so smart persons determine what will become of their financial resources when they die. This can be accomplished by wills, trusts, and life insurance. If a person does not have a will, he needs to draw up one *now.* People do sometimes die in their twenties, thirties, forties, and fifties. If a person does not have a will when he dies, the state determines where his financial resources go after his death. It is a person's duty to his family to determine what happens to his estate when he dies.

Step 5: Write the Spending Plan on Paper

I have already suggested this. Make several copies to keep in different places. Let each member of the family, except small children, have a copy of the plan.

Although there are no "average" individuals, families, or plans, each year various lists of estimated expenditures are drawn up by pollsters and the media.

Possible percentages of income for both single persons and families are projected. A composite for singles would indicate that they spend 25 to 30 percent for housing, 10 to 15 percent for food, 4 to 8 percent for clothing and personal care, 4 to 7 percent for utilities, 1 to 3 percent for insurance, 5 to 7 percent for savings, 10 to 15 percent for a vehicle, and the rest for entertainment and miscellaneous.

The "average" family of four with both parents working may spend 30 percent for housing, 10 to 14 percent for food, 4 to 10 percent for clothing and personal care, 4 to 7 percent for utilities, 3 to 5 percent for insurance, 5 to 7 percent for savings, 8 to 10 percent for vehicle(s), and the remainder for entertainment and miscellaneous.

A retired couple is projected to spend 10-15 percent for housing, 15-20 percent for food, 1-5 percent for clothing and personal care, 15-18 percent for utilities, 1-5 percent for insurance, 1-5 percent for savings, 15-20 percent for medical, and the rest miscellaneous.

One should note a couple of flaws in the above projections. First of all, there is no provision for medical expenses in the first two examples. Second, if a person believes that the Bible teaches tithing (giving 10 percent of one's income to the church), he will be aware that these examples allow nothing for that priority item. The first item in a Christian's budget should be the tithe for the Lord's work and offerings for other causes.

Step 6: Include the Lord's Work in the Budget

Christian stewardship and a biblical life-style include putting aside a sum of money each pay period for the Lord's work. This ought to come first. Many people believe that the minimum amount of money a believer or a believing family should give to the Lord is a tithe. This will be discussed later in this chapter. Each person will need to decide the percentage to give to the Lord when he prepares his budget. Make it the first item. The percentage should not be less than a tithe.

Step 7: Keep Accurate Records

This step is basic and imperative for sound management of financial resources. One will be able to determine how well his spending plan is working and be able to adjust his budget in the future. Accurate records are needed when figuring income tax.

Living on Credit Cards

To some consumers, credit cards are a blessing. Others simply cannot handle them. Credit cards can be an open invitation for a person to overspend his budget. Some have opted to destroy all their credit cards and pay cash for everything. In today's world that calls for more discipline than the average person has, one runs the risk of not being able to handle emergencies.

Before handing a credit card to a sales clerk, make sure the item bought will be staying within your budget. There is no joy when those monthly bills arrive, and they amount to a sum greater than one's entire monthly income. The interest rates on credit cards tend to be rather high, and one can waste money paying interest, unless he consistently takes care of his bills at the end of each month.

Tithing

Tithing means giving 10 percent of one's income to the Lord's work. True income is usually considered the income which the Internal Revenue Service declares a person must pay tax on. There is a biblical basis for tithing. Read the following Scripture passage.

> Will a man rob God? Yet ye have robbed me. But ye say, Wherein have we robbed thee? In tithes and offerings.
>
> Ye are cursed with a curse: for ye have robbed me, even this whole nation.
>
> Bring ye all the tithes into the storehouse, that there may be meat in mine house, and prove me now herewith, saith the Lord of hosts, if I will not open you the windows of heaven, and pour you out a blessing, that there shall not be room enough to receive it (Mal. 3:8-10).

The eighth commandment of the Ten Commandments warns, "Thou shalt not steal" (Ex. 20:15). God spoke through the prophet Malachi that if a person does not tithe he is stealing money belonging to God. It would be misappropriating the financial resources given to that person. Each person is a steward of God and uses what belongs to the Master.

Notice that there are two results mentioned in the verses—a *curse* for those who would rob God and a *blessing* for tithers. The blessing is not necessarily financial. Do not expect to become financially rich as a result of tithing. There is no such guarantee in the Bible, though some who tithe have become wealthy.

Tithing was an honored custom even before the Mosaic Law was instituted. Abraham (then Abram) "gave him (Melchizedek, the king of Salem) a tenth of everything" (Gen. 14:20)—in other words, a tithe. Tithing was a law later given to the nation of Israel. Does it also apply to the church? Many Christians believe that New Testament giving should be at least a tithe, if not more.

Then, the verses mention not only tithing but also "offerings" which are obviously over and above the tithe.

Next, what is the "storehouse" mentioned in verse Malachi 3:10? Many believe it is the local church. Does it include money given for parachurch organizations? Does it include money given to charitable organizations? To which church does the Christian bring his or her tithes and offerings? In Old Testament times, the "storehouse" was in the temple. Where or what is it today? It is not likely to be a building because there can be a local church even if there is no building. The local church is not merely a building. It is a body of believers in Christ who meet together regularly for worship, education, evangelism, missions, and fellowship.

Many pastors of local churches insist that the local church should be the repository for all tithes and that moneys given to parachurch organizations should be additional "offerings," not tithes. For practical purposes, it is a good idea to give a tithe through one's local church. If one feels he cannot tithe through his local church, perhaps he ought to change churches!

Through the years there has been disagreement over this matter, but it seems wise to support one's own congregation with tithes and offerings. Many give their tithes and offerings to parachurch organizations and ministries instead of their own church where they belong. When many members follow that practice, the local church suffers greatly.

This writer has discovered a principle that many others have found. I have previously alluded to it: *There is only one way to be able to afford to tithe. Take the Lord's tithe out of one's income first.*

New Testament Principles of Stewardship

Some do not feel that tithing is a New Testament obligation since it is not specifically mentioned as a commandment in the New Testament. However, refer to the following words of Jesus.

> Woe unto you, scribes and Pharisees, hypocrites! for ye pay tithes of mint and anise and cummin, and have omitted the weightier matters of the law, judgment, mercy, and faith; these ought ye to have done, and not to leave the other undone (Matt. 23:23).

The words of Jesus, "These ought ye to have done," imply that tithing is to be continued indefinitely by the church, as well as by Israel. Yet, tithing is not mentioned in the Epistles of Paul, James, Peter, John, or Jude. Does this tell people that tithing is not for today? No. It may have been that the writers of the New Testament letters never mentioned tithing because it was not a problem in their day. It may have been taken for granted by all the churches that tithing as done by the old Israel—the Jews—was still in effect for the new Israel—the church.

At any rate, what positive, definite teaching is found in the New Testament about the stewardship and management of financial resources? People find such instruction, not necessarily in a systematic form, in a letter the apostle Paul wrote to the Corinthian church. From his instructions to them, people can determine certain principles of New Testament stewardship. They are as follows:

Poverty Is No Excuse for Not Giving

The Macedonian Christians gave generously in spite of their considerable poverty. The result was an abundance of their joy. There is joy in giving even if a person is poor. "How that in a great trial of affliction the abundance of their joy and their deep poverty abounded unto the riches of their liberality" (2 Cor. 8:2).

First Give of Oneself

God wants each person first and gifts second. "This they did, not as we hoped, but first gave their own selves to the Lord, and unto us by the will of God" (2 Cor. 8:5).

Abound in the Grace of Giving

There is an abundance of joy for the person and the family that not only are faithful in other areas of life, but also are committed in giving. "Therefore, as ye abound in every thing, in faith, and utterance, and knowledge, and in all diligence, and in your love to us, see that ye abound in this grace also" (2 Cor. 8:7).

Prove One's Faith by Giving

Profession is no proof of one's faith in Christ. Not even one's regular attendance at church is evidence of the intensity and sincerity of one's faith. But one's giving can help prove the quality of one's faith. "I speak not by commandment, but by occasion of the forwardness of others, and to prove the sincerity of your love" (2 Cor. 8:8).

Giving Is Following Christ

God gave His only Son to die for all the world. Jesus freely offered His life for all. Jesus who was rich, having ownership of the entire universe, became poor for everyone. "For ye know the grace of our Lord Jesus Christ, that, though he was rich, yet for your sakes he became poor, that ye through his poverty might be rich (2 Cor. 8:9).

Giving Should Be Done Willingly

People often write a check for their taxes reluctantly, forgetting that they probably garnered their money's worth. Giving to the Lord should be done willingly, realizing what He has done for people, seeing what He is still doing for them and continuing today. "For if there be first a willing mind, it is accepted according to that a man hath, and not according to that he hath not" (2 Cor. 8:12).

One Reaps What One Sows

A farmer's crops are determined by the seeds he sows, assuming that he has sufficient rain. If he plants few crops, he receives a small return. If he plants many acres of seed, he expects a large crop. "This I say, he which soweth sparingly shall reap also sparingly; and he which soweth bountifully shall reap also bountifully" (2 Cor. 9:6).

Give Joyfully

There is no joy in giving if people give only because they must. There is exhilaration in giving because one loves the Lord and wants to further His cause. The more one gives, the greater is his joy. "Every man according as he purposeth in his heart, so let him give; not grudgingly, or of necessity; for God loveth a cheerful giver" (2 Cor. 9:7).

The word *cheerful* in this verse comes from a Greek

word that means hilarious. God loves a hilarious giver. What does that mean? Read the following example.

A pastor has taken the usual morning offering. He is led of the Lord to take up another offering. He may or may not have the church's permission to do this. In responding to this additional offering, one says to himself, *Amen. Praise the Lord! Now I'll have another opportunity to give to the Lord!* Or would a person complain, "All this church wants is money, money, money." The first response is hilarious, joyful giving. The latter response is giving grudgingly.

Giving Is Thanking God for Jesus

When a person compares what God has done for him, what Jesus did for him on the cross of Calvary, and what His Holy Spirit does for him daily, giving to the Lord is a joyful response. "Thanks be unto God for his unspeakable gift" (2 Cor. 9:15).

7
The Use of Talents and Spiritual Gifts

I was preaching for a church revival meeting in Virginia. The pastor discovered that I could play the organ. He asked me to play an organ solo one night. I told him I would rather not because I seldom practiced. He responded by reminding me that if I did not use a talent or ability I had, I would lose it. It would be like not using one's muscles and thus letting them atrophy.

Ever since that day, I have used my musical talent in every church where I have served. Talents and spiritual gifts are meant to be used, not neglected.

The Difference Between Talents and Spiritual Gifts

Webster defines a talent as the natural endowment of a person or a special creative or artistic aptitude. In other words, it is an inborn ability to do something. A spiritual gift is given to a person by the Holy Spirit. It is not an ability that one is born with. As a talent is a *natural* endowment, a spiritual gift is a *divine* endowment. It is possible for the Holy Spirit to combine a spiritual gift with an already given natural endowment. Thus, the ability is heightened by the addition of the Holy Spirit.

The enjoyment of life means using one's abilities and gifts through living out one's philosophy of life and strategy for living. People use their abilities and gifts, thus being enabled to reach the goals the Lord has led them to choose. Failing to use these natural talents and God-given spiritual gifts is to miss the greatest joys of life.

The Bible on Talents

The word *talent* as defined earlier is not found in the Bible. In Scripture, *talent* means money. Places in the New Testament where the word is found are Matthew 18; 24; 25; 28; and Revelation 16. The word *talent* comes from a Greek word which refers, not to an inborn ability, but to a weight or an amount of money. Jesus used the word in his Olivet discourse (see Matt. 24 and 25) concerning an amount of money given to someone.

In this discourse, one person received five talents, another two, and another only one. The first two persons invested their talents wisely for a good return. The person who was given only one talent hid it, instead of investing it. Displeasure was expressed to this person for not investing (using) his talent.

Even though the "talent" in Jesus' story is an amount of money, people can draw a spiritual application by looking at the parallel to their inborn abilities and gifts. Some people are fortunate in having as many as five talents and/or spiritual gifts. They are expected to use them all. Some have only two talents and/or spiritual gifts. They are expected to use them. Perhaps a person has only one talent or spiritual gift. He should not hide it. He is challenged to use it and invest it. By using whatever talents and spiritual gifts one has, he can reach his goals and enjoy life. Each person will be held accountable to the Lord for the use of his abilities and spiritual gifts.

The Bible on Spiritual Gifts

Spiritual gifts are first mentioned in Romans 12 where a partial list is given by the apostle Paul to the church at Rome.

> Having then gifts differing according to the grace that is given to us whether prophecy, let us prophesy according to the proportion of faith;
> Or ministry, let us wait on our ministering; or he that teacheth, on teaching;
> Or he that exhorteth, on exhortation; he that giveth, let him do it with simplicity; he that ruleth, with diligence; he that showeth mercy, with cheerfulness (Rom. 12:6-8).

The following gifts were mentioned in the Scripture passage:

- *Prophecy.* A probable reference to preaching through comforting, exhorting, and encouraging.
- *Ministry.* A probable reference to either service to God and others in general or to a specific church office, such as being a deacon.
- *Teaching.* Any form of teaching, but especially to teaching the Word of God; as, for instance, a Sunday School teacher.
- *Exhortation.* Another reference to speaking to others.
- *Giving.* Some have a special gift of generous giving.
- *Ruling.* A reference to leadership.
- *Showing Mercy.* While this should be done by all people, some have a special gift for this.

Another reference to spiritual gifts is found in Paul's Letter to the Ephesians. Chapter 4, verse 7 refers to spiritual gifts as the gifts "of Christ." "He gave some, apostles; and some prophets; and some, evangelists; and some, pastors and teachers" (Eph. 4:11).

Several gifts are noted in this Scripture verse. They refer to specific offices in the church (the body of Christ). The gifts included are:

- *Apostles*. The original twelve disciples, the disciples who took Judas's place, and all later apostles; that is, those who have "seen the Lord." Today one might call them missionaries.
- *Prophets*. Preachers of the Word of God, not just those who predict the future. (Even the Old Testament prophets did more preaching against sin than they did predicting the future.)
- *Evangelists*. Those whose main ministry is to win people to the Lord. They are itinerant preachers.
- *Pastors* and *Teachers*. Probably two words are used here to describe one office. Every pastor is supposed to be a teacher.

In the following verse, we are told the purpose for a person receiving gifts: "For the perfecting of the saints, for the work of the ministry, for the edifying of the body of Christ" (Eph. 4:12). Obviously, the two lists of spiritual gifts are partial rather than complete. Whatever spiritual gift is needed in any place or by any person, the Holy Spirit can provide that gift to the person of His (the Holy Spirit's) choice.

A crucial scriptural passage is found in the apostle Paul's first Letter to the Corinthians in which three entire chapters discuss spiritual gifts. Refer to 1 Corinthians 12; 13; and 14. Chapter 12 describes the spiritual gifts in the church that are to be devoted to the service of God and to the ministry of the Word of God. Chapter 13 tells how the gifts of the Spirit should be used. It states that these gifts should be governed by (*agape*) love. Chapter 14 speaks of prophecy (preaching) as being the greatest of the gifts.

A third partial list of spiritual gifts is given:

> For to one is given by the Spirit the word of wisdom; to another the word of knowledge by the same Spirit;
>
> To another faith by the same Spirit; to another the gifts of healing by the same Spirit;
>
> To another the working of miracles; to another prophecy; to another discerning of spirits; to another divers kinds of tongues; to another the interpretation of tongues (1 Cor. 12:8-10).

What do these gifts mean?

- *Wisdom.* The ability to use knowledge. Good judgment.
- *Knowledge.* The ability to gain knowledge.
- *Faith.* A special ability to trust God.
- *Healing.* All types of healing—mental, physical, emotional, psychological—may be involved. Many believers have this gift. God uses the medical profession, plus some outside of that profession who have this gift.
- *Miracle Working.* An ability empowered to some to perform miracles.
- *Prophecy.* Preaching and to some extent predicting.
- *Discerning of Spirits.* Being able to understand the true from the false and the spiritual from the unspiritual—special insight into spiritual surroundings and conditions.
- *Tongues.* Paul considered this one of the lesser gifts (see 1 Cor. 14), yet the gift was real in New Testament days. Many believe such a gift is still

operative today.

- *Interpretation*. Some people are able to understand those who speak in tongues. They can interpret or translate.

Who Determines What Gifts a Person Has?

Undoubtedly, it is good that people cannot select their own spiritual gifts. Most people would probably choose the most spectacular ones rather than those that are most needed. There is only one person who is fully qualified to choose the spiritual gifts people are given, and that is the Lord. The Bible teaches that God determines how many gifts people are to receive and which ones they will be. "But all these worketh that one and the selfsame Spirit, dividing to every man severally as he will" (1 Cor. 12:11). The "all these" refers to the spiritual gifts mentioned in the previous verses. Natural talents are determined by our genes, by our parents, grandparents, great grandparents, and so forth. However, our spiritual gifts are not handed down by our ancestors but by God.

List your natural talents such as artistic or mechanical abilities in music, art, carpentry, or mechanics. Then, list one or more spiritual gifts you believe the Holy Spirit has given. A person may have only one gift. One may have two, three, or more gifts. We are to use both our talents and our spiritual gifts to glorify God (not self). Thus, in this process of glorifying God, people *enjoy life to the fullest*.

8
Health and Fitness

How we may enjoy life is partly based on the condition of one's health. So each person should consider how he or she can achieve an optimum of health and physical fitness. How a person cares for his health should be determined by his philosophy of life, strategy for living, goals, and how he can live for God's glory.

Certainly, poor health ushers sorrow into one's life, and it is generally assumed that reasonably good health enables one to enjoy life more. While a serious, painful (even terminal) illness can glorify God, radiant health can bring Him glory and give joy to people. Reaching long-term goals will probably be difficult if one is in poor health or if, by reason of poor health, one dies young or in middle age. Achieving and maintaining optimum health and fitness are not passing fads, not selfish desires, but avenues of glorifying God and allowing us to enjoy life with God's service in mind.

The Bible on Health

The Bible says very little about health and physical fitness, especially in the New Testament, but it does speak at length in the Book of Proverbs in the Old Testament. Note the following Scriptures on the subject of *alcohol*:

> Listen, my son, and be wise,
> And direct your heart in the way.
> Do not be with heavy drinkers of wine,
> Or with gluttonous eaters of meat;
> For the heavy drinker and the glutton
>   will come to poverty,
> And drowsiness will clothe a man with rags
>   (Prov. 23:19-21, NASB).

These verses do not speak directly to poor health as the result of drunkenness and gluttony, but people realize today that alcoholism and overindulgence in food can shorten lives. Note these verses:

> Who has woe? Who has sorrow?
> Who has contentions? Who has complaining?
> Who has wounds without cause?
> Who has redness of eyes?
> Those who linger long over wine,
> Those who go to taste mixed wine.
> Do not look on the wine when it is red,
> When it sparkles in the cup,
> When it goes down smoothly;
> At the last it bites like a serpent,
> And stings like a viper.
> Your eyes will see strange things,
> And your mind will utter perverse things
>   (Prov. 23:29-33, NASB).

Note the following verses on the subject of *food*.

> When you sit down to dine with a ruler,
> Consider carefully what is before you;
> And put a knife to your throat,
> If you are a man of great appetite.
> Do not desire his delicacies,
> For it is deceptive food
>   (Prov. 23:1-3, NASB).

Don't these verses sound like today's admonitions not to eat wrong kinds of food such as: saturated fats, too much sugar and salt, high-cholesterol foods, and the like?

Enjoying Life in Terminal Illness

People have declared that good health is a factor in glorifying God and in enjoying life to the fullest. But suppose a person is suffering from a terminal illness? Is joy still possible under such suffering and pain, and with the realization that one has only a short while to live? Remember, in an earlier chapter, the difference between happiness and joy was noted. Happiness is hardly possible in terminal illness, but joy is. Joy is possible because it is a fruit of the Spirit, not of circumstances.

Most people will someday suffer terminal illness of either short or long duration. There may be pain and suffering, but there is also the help of the Holy Spirit even more than ever. Terminal illness is the door into the greatest enjoyment possible for the Christian—heaven.

Diet and Diets

This writer has no special qualifications to suggest diets, and this book need not suggest them anyway, since the world is full of diets and diet books. However, I want to emphasize a point: the time to be careful about what you eat is not after you get sick or when you reach middle or old age. The time to watch carefully what you eat is *now*.

I feel that the doctor's office is the best place to discover a diet. The doctor may not be specially trained in nutrition, but he/she can give a person the proper diet

to keep his or her weight under control and cholesterol
and blood sugar down. Admittedly, there are nutrition-
ists, clinics, and special programs which can help.

Exercising for Optimum Health

The place to find out about an exercise program is
also in the doctor's office It is certain that everyone
needs exercise, unless the doctor advises otherwise. It
may be jogging, walking, weight lifting, or aerobics.
Whatever it is, people ought to begin it as soon as they
recognize the need for it, and the doctor has prescribed
it.

Each person can walk more and drive less. Walk up
and down stairs, instead of using elevators and escala-
tors. People can park their cars farther from where
they are going, instead of as close as possible to their
destination.

Muscles that are not used will eventually become un-
usable. The time to begin a program of daily exercise is
today, after checking with one's doctor.

Drugs—Prescription and Over-the-Counter

Some people, including some athletes, have wrongly
believed that the best way to win—to enjoy life to the
fullest—is to get a lift from some drugs. Eventually, the
use of these unprescribed drugs are counterproductive
to the enjoyment of life. There is a time for their use,
which is when they are prescribed by a doctor.

A lot of money is wasted on over-the-counter, nonpre-
scription drugs that may not be needed, especially if
people would watch what they eat, how much they eat,
and get the exercise they need. To some degree, all
drugs are poison and should be taken only when
necessary.

Divine Healing

Suppose one lost his health due to his own wrong living or because of causes entirely unrelated to his lifestyle. Not all illness is the result of our sins, though some are, perhaps more than we think. Can one then ask the Lord to heal him? Can one go to a person who claims to have the ability to heal him, even though he is not a member of the medical profession? Will God heal him in answer to faith and prayer?

A classic passage in the New Testament on divine/faith healing is found in James 5. Examine this Scripture passage carefully.

> Is any sick among you? let him call for the elders of the church; and let them pray over him, anointing him with oil in the name of the Lord:
> And the prayer of faith shall save the sick, and the Lord shall raise him up; and if he have committed sins, they shall be forgiven him.
> Confess your faults one to another, and pray one for another, that ye may be healed. The effectual fervent prayer of a righteous man availeth much (Jas. 5:14-16).

First, note that when a person is sick (and this undoubtedly refers to a serious illness), he or she is to notify the elders—perhaps pastors or older leaders in the church. In most churches, this is seldom done. People notify the doctor and then perhaps the pastor. The pastor and church leaders ought to hear about the sickness immediately. Often, pastors are criticized for not visiting the sick when no one has notified him. Each person assumed that someone else had done this. The pastor, if he heard about it at all, was the last to know.

Second, the pastor or elder is to go where the sick

person is, either to the home or the hospital.

Third, the pastor or elder is to pray for the sick. Nowhere are pastors told that they have the right to demand (as some faith healers have done) that God heal the sick person. Only God can demand, not human beings. The prayers of the pastor can request healing, if it is the will of God for the glory of God and for the best interests of all concerned.

Fourth, James instructed his readers to anoint the seriously ill person with oil. When I pastored my first church, I was asked by one member to anoint a very sick patient with oil. I refused, saying that this procedure was no longer necessary in this age of modern medicine. I believe that was a mistake. If I were asked to do it today, I would purchase some olive oil and anoint the sick, even if I did not feel it was necessary or helpful. Such an act is preferable to alienating a person who believes that he should anoint the seriously ill with oil, even today. In earlier days of the apostle James, oil could be used as a soothing agent, but today other medicines assist the body's healing powers. (It might be noted, however, that in the Bible oil is sometimes a symbol of the Holy Spirit.)

Then James spoke of the prayer of faith and its resultant healing of the sick. People cannot build a doctrine (such as the doctrine of prayer) on just one Scripture verse. People must also employ all that the rest of the Bible teaches on the subject.

In 1 John 5:14-15, people read that prayers will receive an affirmative answer only if what they ask for is in the will of God. And they cannot assume that God's will is always to heal a sick person. Also note in the passage of Scripture the relationship of sin to sickness. Not all sickness is the definite result of one's sins. If a person is an alcoholic, then his or her liver suffers. If a person smokes, his or her lungs, stomach, and heart suffer. If people eat too many of the wrong foods, their overall health is affected. If people live with others who smoke, they may contract lung cancer, just as the one who smokes can develop cancer or emphysema.

James wrote that forgiveness for our sins is a requirement. Nobody can enjoy life by carrying around the weight of guilt and sin. The remedy, James declared, is to confess one's sins. Finally, James noted that the fervent prayers of *righteous* people avail much. Note two facts here: (1) Only the prayers of the righteous prevail. (2) They avail much, but not for everything. There is no guarantee that a person's prayers for health will always receive an affirmative answer.

In summary, to enjoy life to the fullest and to live for the glory of God, people should do what is necessary for the preservation of their physical, mental, and emotional health. With good health, people are more likely to reach their goals.

9
Christian Social Life

A life without at least a minimum of recreation and entertainment could end like the proverb says, "All work and no play makes Jack a dull boy." Webster defines *recreation* as to restore or refresh or as refreshment of strength and spirits after toil. It partly comes from the root word for *create*, and the prefix *re* gives it the meaning to create again or to re-create.

No doubt plenty that is called recreation does not restore or refresh people but actually has the opposite effect. Many workers returning from a weekend of what they think is recreation are not restored to become more productive, creative workers.

Webster says that *entertainment* is synonymous with *amusement*. People can divide amusements into those that are helpful and those that are hurtful. The word *amuse* comes from two words—*muse*, meaning to think, coupled with the prefix *a* which means not to think. Does this imply that to be amused is to engage in that which keeps people from thinking?

Recreation and entertainment must somehow be related to one's enjoyment of life to the fullest. Apparently, people's bodies, minds, and spirits need some healthy, moral form of diversion from the routine of their daily work. But, again, some forms of recreation and entertainment harm the body, dull the mind, and blunt the spirit.

Choosing to engage only in those forms of recreation and entertainment that are positive and improve the quality of life, people ought to have some guidelines. To begin with, recreation and entertainment should fit in with one's philosophy of life and strategy for living. These activities should also glorify God because true enjoyment is related directly to living for Him.

What does the Bible say about recreation and entertainment? Practically nothing directly but a great deal indirectly. Note the following Scriptures:

> What? know ye not that your body is the temple of the Holy Ghost which is in you, which ye have of God, and ye are not your own?
> For ye are bought with a price; therefore glorify God in your body, and in your spirit, which are God's (1 Cor. 6:19-20).

Could a person conclude, then, that any form of recreation or entertainment that harms the body must be excluded? "All things are lawful for me, but all things are not expedient: all things are lawful for me, but all things edify not" (1 Cor. 10:23). The following verse is similar to that verse except for the last part: "All things are lawful unto me, but all things are not expedient: all things are lawful for me, but I will not be brought under the power of any" (1 Cor. 6:12) Does this tell people, then, that some forms of recreation and entertainment, while perfectly legal and permissible even for Christians, should be excluded?

Finally, remember a basic verse of Scripture: "Whether therefore ye eat, or drink, or whatsoever ye do, do all to the glory of God" (1 Cor. 10:31). The instruc-

tion is that recreation and entertainment are essential
to physical, mental, and emotional health, but people
should limit their recreation and entertainment to
forms which are pleasing to God. Those are the only
ones that will present full enjoyment to their lives.

How to Determine Right and Wrong

How does one determine right from wrong? That is a
potent subject regardless of one's age or the era in
which he lives. The written Word of God and the leadership of the Holy Spirit are first and foremost in the
Christian's decision-making. Yet, there are still per-
plexing questions in every generation. In Paul's day
there was a hot controversy over the eating of meat. It
involved the question of whether one should eat meat
that might have been offered to heathen idols and then
sold to an unsuspecting Christian in the marketplace.

I believe the late ethicist T. B. Maston wrote perhaps,
next to the Bible, the best book on making decisions in-
volving right and wrong. It was *Right or Wrong.*[1] I also
appreciated Bernard Ramm's *The Right, the Good, and
the Happy.*[2]

The first book deals more directly with the subject of
recreation and entertainment, but the latter contains
an excellent study of the Christian in a world of distort-
ed values.

Maston presents some excellent principles to guide
people in their decisions about recreation and entertainment. The first principle concerns the various levels of living. Maston lists four levels of living: (1) the
instinctive in which people live more or less like ani-
mals, (2) the customary in which people do what most
of the community approves of, (3) the conscience in
which people follow the rule of let their conscience be

their guide, and (4) the Christian in which their recreation and entertainment are determined by biblical principles (such as quoted in the previous section).

Maston's second principle deals with the stewardship of a Christian, which was covered earlier in this book in Chapters 6 and 7. He speaks about the use of material possessions, the care of one's body, the effect on personalities, the amount of time one spends in recreation and entertainment, and the influence that forms of recreation and entertainment have on others, especially on the non-Christians or on weak Christians.

Maston's third principle relates to the sources of any recreation or form of entertainment being wrong for the Christian. He says some forms of recreation or entertainment are wrong by "association." Should Christians be seen gambling in Atlantic City? Should they be seen in a building that is suspected of shady business dealings? Should they play pool in a place where known immoral people gather?

Maston says that some forms of recreation and entertainment, though perhaps not inherently wrong, may be considered improper for the Christian because of the attitude of others, such as parents and teachers. Finally, on this third principle, Maston reminds people that moral principles, as found in the Bible, are absolute and unchangeable, not relative and determined by the times in which people live.

Maston's fourth principle deals with determinants of right. Who determines what is right? A church member said to me years ago, "Nobody's going to tell me what to do or not to do." He was wrong. That is exactly what God *is* going to do.

Maston mentions three determinants of right: (1) the individual (who may not be objectively qualified to decide and yet eventually will), (2) the group (if so, which group?), and (3) God (He is the final judge on right and wrong. His judgment is perfect.).

Maston's fifth principle concerns three questions about choice of recreation or form of entertainment. He says people must first ask about its effect on *them* (on their bodies, minds, and spiritual lives). Second, people must ask about its effect on *others* (since Christians are to witness to others and be a positive influence on them). Third, people must ask about its effect on the *kingdom of God*.

Maston's sixth principle suggests that people apply three tests to their choice of recreation or entertainment. First, *must it be done in secret*? "This is the condemnation that light is come into the world, and men loved darkness rather than light, because their deeds were evil" (John 3:19). If it must be done in secret, it may be wrong. Second, the test of *universality*. If everyone did it, would it be OK? Would it be all right for one's mother, father, sister, or brother to do it? What about one's pastor? Third, the test of *prayer*. Can a person pray about this form of recreation or entertainment and ask God to bless it?

Maston's seventh and final principle is to suggest that there are three *sources of light* (help) in determining right and wrong. They are help from *within*, from *without* (Christian counselors, for instance), and from *above* (from God).

Recreation and Entertainment that Can Be Harmful

Gambling. Can a Christian gamble? Relate Christian stewardship to this form of entertainment or attempt to get something for nothing. Is gambling often associated with the criminal element, even if done by a government body? Does the Bible state that people should earn their income by work (the biblical work ethic)? Should people expect to get something for nothing? What is the effect of gambling on others (the poor, the weak Christian, and so forth)? Can a person pray and ask God to help him or her to win? Is gambling addictive?

Smoking. Does smoking harm the body (lungs, heart, stomach, and so forth)? Is it frequently a cause of lung cancer and/or emphysema? Does it use an inordinate amount of money (stewardship principle)? Does it offend others who do not want to inhale the smoke that can cause cancer and annoy them? Have health authorities warned against it?

Drinking alcohol. What affect does the consumption of alcohol have on the body? Large amounts of it are harmful to the liver and the brain. Even small amounts have contributed to automobile accidents, some of which result in someone's death. What does drinking alcoholic beverages do to one's testimony, to the non-Christian, and to the weak Christian? What effect does alcohol consumption have on the mind? The spiritual life?

Using other drugs. This refers to drugs that are not prescribed by doctors. What is the effect of unprescribed, illegal drugs on the body? Cocaine? Marijuana? LSD? How do they affect rational thinking? What do they do to the spiritual lives of drug addicts? To their families? Considering, too, the high cost of illegal drugs, what about the stewardship principle? These are soul-searching questions.

Notes

1. T. B. Maston, *Right or Wrong* (Nashville: Broadman Press, 1955).

2. Bernard Ramm, *The Right, the Good, and the Happy* (Waco, TX: Word Books, 1971).

10
Your Family

We are living in a secular age. I am not alone in believing that certain adherents of secular humanism are attempting to destroy America's family life. Yet, family life was ordained of God from the beginning. Believe it or not, many feel that children's morals should be determined by the public school rather than by parents and the church. Others are redefining a family as two or more people living together rather than the traditional family of two married people and children if they have any, plus the extended family like relatives who live with the family.

According to the Bible, children belong to God first and then their parents, not to the government or school system. The family is the ideal—if not the only way—to rear children. The rearing of children in an institution, even one that is Christian, is not the ideal, of course. Children need the guidance of parents, if that is possible. God originally intended men and women to marry and bear children. Certainly we recognize that many couples are not able to have children. Because of unfortunate circumstances, many children are in foster homes or institutions.

The full enjoyment of life for many people includes living in a family or being married and bearing children. However, this is *not* to indicate that people who choose the single life (or are forced into it by circumstances) cannot enjoy life to the fullest. Nor does it say that a woman cannot experience the fullness of life without bearing a child. The church, which usually consists mostly of families, has finally started to provide educational and recreational facilities for singles. Many churches employ a minister to singles.

The Bible does not condone a man and woman "living together" without the commitment of marriage. God intended marriage to be a lifelong relationship.

Relating all this to the theme of this book, the decision whether to marry or stay single is each person's choice and should be determined by his or her philosophy of life, strategy for living, and the glory of God.

Weddings

When weddings are performed in a church setting (in fact, all weddings, wherever they are conducted), they ought to be worship experiences. Too often today's ceremonies are like staged spectacles. This is my own opinion, but I feel the music is often too secular.

All factors relating to weddings should, as in all matters, be determined by one's philosophy of life, strategy for living, and the glorification of God. Weddings should not glorify the bride and groom. They should exalt Jesus Christ and should bring honor and glory to God who ordained marriage. Weddings should be Christ centered.

Just as the wedding should be consistent with one's philosophy of life, strategy for living, and what will glorify God, so should the marriage. Marriage ought to be one of the most enjoyable of life's experiences, and it can be, if *both* people are living for God and for each other, not merely for self-satisfaction.

Divorce

According to the Bible, especially the words of Jesus, God intended the marriage relationship to be monogamous and permanent. Anything less deviates from God's standard. Yet, knowing the frailties of humankind, it is the belief of the writer that the Bible permits two possible reasons why a divorce may be granted: (1) the adultery or fornication of one or both partners and (2) the departure of an unbeliever from a believer. And, it is the belief of the writer, that when a divorce has been obtained on biblical grounds, the divorced believer has a moral right to remarry.

The words of Jesus concerning divorce are found in Matthew 19:3-12. One verse is quoted here: "I say unto you, Whosoever shall put away his wife, except it be for fornication, and shall marry another, committeth adultery: and whoso marrieth her which is put away doth commit adultery" (v. 9). Jesus did not discuss divorce in any of His statements described by Paul in 1 Corinthians 7. The apostle Paul wrote: "But if the unbelieving depart, let him depart. A brother or sister is not under bondage in such cases: but God hath called us to peace" (v. 15). The "bondage" obviously refers to the marriage bonds. However, the believer is not to be the one who deserts the unbeliever.

Granting a divorce from one's spouse, under the principle stated in 1 Corinthians 7:15, is a permission, not a requirement. Any remarriage should be made with the clear understanding that the divorce process should not be repeated. Most marriages should and can be successful if both spouses accept long-term Christian counseling.

Family Worship

Considering one's Christian philosophy of life, strategy for living, and life-style for the glory of God, family worship should be obligatory. The best time to begin family worship is as soon as people are married. Let children be active in family worship as soon as they are able to speak. Use family worship to instruct the family in biblical doctrine and morals, to teach the children to read the Bible and to pray, and to help unify the family. Individual and private worship are as important as family worship, and these will be discussed in the next chapter.

11
Your Devotional Life

Devotional life refers to one's private praying, reading of the Bible and devotional books, and meditation. It is probable that a large percentage of Christians have no devotional life whatsoever. They neither feel a need for it nor believe that they have time for it. Yet, they have ample time for TV, sports, trips, games, you name it.

One's devotional life is the dynamic of the Christian life, a source of power, and fully as important as public worship. A person's devotional life should be consistent with his walk for the Lord.

Private Prayer

In this technological age, I am surprised that someone has not tried to come up with computers and software designed to do their praying for them. Prayer rooted and grounded in God is not a "snap," so many would like to have a modern "prayer wheel." Lazy Christians could wave good night to God before going to bed. They would no longer have to "waste" precious time praying, no longer have to wear out their knees on the hard floor, crying out to the Lord for help. I think many modern Christians would love to type into the computer the appropriate prayers for all possible occasions. Why, when they needed to pray, all they'd have to do is to give a command to the computer which would then print out their prayers for God to read, or it would pray in an audible voice, as some computers can do. What a timesaver!

Such a computer with prayer software would enable people to dispatch in a few moments as many prayers as they could pray in hours. When mass produced, the cost of such a computer and software would be affordable for every home and church. It would become as indispensable as a refrigerator. No Christian home should be without one.

By now I trust you realize I am being facetious. There is one wrinkle to be ironed out in this prayer computer and software. It will not work! God would not read the printout or listen to any spoken words from it. In other words, there has not been, is not now, and will not be a substitute for direct communication with God through prayer. Some say, "Prayer is phony." Some have even tried it and complained it doesn't work. No doubt some praying is phony and hypocritical. Praying is phony when the pray-ers are phony.

Others think of prayer as a religious duty, comparable to some Christians as mowing the lawn, washing the dishes, or dusting the furniture. Others think of prayer as being like a spare tire—something to use in emergencies only. Others think of it as a form of magic: "I prayed for healing, and I didn't get it." "I prayed for my husband to quit drinking; he didn't." "I prayed to pass my exams; I flunked."

Therefore, some whine, "You tell me to pray, and I've done it. But what good is it? It doesn't work." Some have the idea that praying is like putting a quarter in a vending machine and expecting it to deliver a predetermined item.

So, prayer for some Christians is a necessary duty, a burden. They think that maybe it will work and that it is something they are supposed to believe in and do. Because they don't do it, they feel guilty about it. However, in times of trouble, they do all kinds of praying, hoping for an answer.

In this materialistic, humanistic age, can they still believe in and practice the art of prayer? The biblical hero Job asked a piercing question about payer: "What profit should we have, if we pray unto him?" (21:15).

Regulating One's Prayer Life

J. Paul Carleton wrote a book *Rejoicing in Prayer* in 1949 (it has been out of print for years), but the ideas from it have influenced my prayer and meditation.

A person's prayer life should be *regulated*. First, it should be regulated as to *time*.

When Should a Person Pray?

The time to pray should be according to the individual's situation. Many feel that the best time to pray is in the morning, in the same way as many consider the morning meal (breakfast) the most important meal of the day. The time schedule of some Americans, who roll out of bed at the last minute and rush off to work, having nothing to eat or drink until a coffee break, does not allow for a morning prayer time. Some prefer the afternoon or night. What counts most of all is that you set up a definite time and try to stick with it.

If you really want to start the day with prayer, the answer is simple. Get up earlier. First, go to bed earlier. Turn off the television sooner. Which is more important, television or morning communication with the

Lord?

The Bible says, "In the morning, rising up a great while before day, he went out, and departed into a solitary place, and there prayed" (Mark 1:35).

How Often Should a Person Pray?

A person should pray as often as he or she feels necessary to live a Christian life. Certainly that means at least daily. The Bible speaks of the prophet Daniel: "Now when Daniel knew that the writing was signed, he went into his house; and his windows being opened in his chamber toward Jerusalem, he kneeled upon his knees three times a day, and prayed, and gave thanks . . . as he did aforetime" (6:10). King David also spoke about the question of how often to pray. "Evening, and morning, and at noon, will I pray, and cry aloud; and he shall hear my voice" (Ps. 55:17).

How many times a day should one pray? How many times a day does one eat? How many times a day does one need spiritual food? Or does one need to talk with God?

In my first pastorate, many of my parishioners were dairy farmers. They arose at 4:00 a.m. to milk their cows. So, I decided, if they could get up at 4:00 in the morning to begin their day's work, as their pastor I would do the same. I'd arise at 4:00 a.m. to read the Bible and pray. I did it *for two mornings*. Then I went back to getting up at 6:00 a.m.

How Long Should a Person Pray?

A person should pray as long as is necessary. If a person can accomplish that in five minutes, why spend time praying for hours? That's a big "if," isn't it? Pray as long as is necessary for one to reach the goals he or she set forth in his or her strategy for living. Pray as long as the Holy Spirit leads you to pray, and the Holy Spirit will also understand when it is time for you to leave for work or an appointment—but remember that your appointment for prayer is strategic in your spiritual life.

The Bible reports Jesus spent all night in prayer on several occasions. I can remember how guilty I felt as I read about how some people spend hours in prayer as compared to my meager fifteen minutes or less. I read of a man named Payson who wore grooves into hardwood boards where his knees pressed so long and hard.

Marquis DeRenty ordered his servant to call him from his devotions in half an hour. As the servant later saw the marquis praying, he did not want to disturb him. After three and a half hours, the servant finally mustered the courage to interrupt his master's praying. DeRenty commented, "How short that half hour was." Many people sing the hymn "Sweet Hour of Prayer" and enjoy singing it, but how often do people pray for an hour?

No doubt there are times when people need to pray over an extended time, meaning that they'd need to rise early in the morning. Jesus prayed all night on several occasions, but His Model Prayer takes only about a minute or two to pray. So, pray as long as you need in order to do God's will for your life.

Where Should a Person Pray?

The teaching of the Lord is to pray alone often, which is sometimes difficult to do. Jesus went alone, apart from His disciples and others, to talk with the Father. He said, "But thou, when thou prayest, enter into thy closet; and when thou hast shut thy door, pray to thy

Father which is in secret, and thy Father which seeth in secret shall reward thee openly" (Matt. 6:6). The Greek word for *closet* refers to an inner chamber, a place where one can be alone. Jesus practiced what He taught: "In the morning, rising up a great while before day, he went out, and departed into a solitary place, and there prayed" (Mark 1:35). Of course, Jesus prayed in all kinds of situations—He prayed alone, in public, with the disciples, with large crowds, and with small groups.

Receiving from One's Prayer Life

People have every right to expect definite results from their praying. Some disagree with that statement. They believe that the only result of praying is an emotional and psychological lift instead of what Jesus said, "Ask, and it shall be give you; seek, and ye shall find; knock, and it shall be opened unto you" (Matt. 7:7). Some paraphrase their Bibles to read something like this: "Ask, and you shall feel good; seek, and your soul will be exercised, your spirits lifted; knock, and get an emotional high." But, according to what Jesus taught, people sometimes have the right to gauge the effectiveness of their prayers by the definite results they bring. What results? Does prayer really change things? If a person believes the Bible, it does. If a person has experienced answers to his or her prayers, he knows that prayer can and does often change things.

But there are some prayers that would be a waste of time to pray. Do not pray such prayers as: "Dear God, make Boston the capital of Virginia." Do not pray for God to contradict His nature. Do not pray for Him to do what the Bible claims He will never do. Do not let prayers be of the nature that asks God to make a four-cornered triangle or a square circle.

What a person does pray for will be determined by his or her concept of prayer. Prayer is a two-way communication between a person and God. It is not like a magic wand by which a person receives what he or she wants. Ben Franklin quipped, "If man could have half his wishes, he would double his troubles." That could be the case with some people's praying. Prayer is not like an Aladdin's lamp, nor is it like a computer that one programs to spew forth results or a printout.

Prayer may change things and people, if God wills changes to take place. But does prayer change *God*? Will God change His mind because of one's prayers? He will *not*! Prayer will not change the mind or the decision of God. Thank God for that! God's mind never needs to be changed. His decisions are always right the first time. When God makes up His mind, what He has decided is always correct.

It is possible that God may decide to answer a person's prayer, not because He has changed His mind or altered His decision but, rather, because He planned to give him or her what he or she prayed for anyway. So, prayer is *not* bending God's will to meet one's own will. True prayer *is* bending one's will to God's. Read that sentence again and again.

Read again Jesus' statement: "Ask, and it shall be given you; seek, and ye shall find; knock, and it shall be opened unto you" (Matt. 7:7). This discussion is about getting results from praying. This being so, it is imperative that, if one wants definite results, one prays for definite things, people, and actions.

The following list gives some examples of how *not* to pray:

- "Lord, bless all those for whom I should pray."

- "Lord, bless all the missionaries."
- "Lord, bless the pastor."
- "Lord, save souls."
- "Lord, forgive me my sins."

The following is a list of some examples of how one *should* pray definitely:

- "Lord, bless Mrs. Smith next door who is having surgery today. Guide the hands of her surgeon and if it be Your will, bring her back to health again."
- "Lord, bless Rev. and Mrs. Jones, as they serve You in Nigeria. Meet their physical, financial, and spiritual needs. Help them not to be discouraged."
- "Lord, help me by my words and deeds to witness to Mrs. Johnston about her need of Christ and the church."
- "Lord, forgive me for yelling at my son. Help me always to be kind but firm when I need to be."

As one prays definitely for specific results, remember that the definite results one receives may not be what is wanted but what the Lord knows is best. I cannot find the source of this poem, but I picked it up somewhere over the years:

I asked for strength, that I might achieve.

I was made weak, that I might learn humbly to obey.

I asked for help that I might do greater things.

I was given infirmity that I might do better things.

I asked for power that I might have the praise of men.

I was given weakness that I might feel the need of God.

I asked for all things that I might enjoy life.

I was given life that I might enjoy all things.

I got nothing that I asked for but everything I needed.

Almost, despite myself, my unspoken prayers were answered.

I am, among men, most richly blessed.

The poem tells us something about receiving definite results from definite praying and yet not always getting exactly what we asked for.

Rejoicing in One's Prayer Life

Returning to an earlier thought in this chapter, note that many regard prayer as a necessary religious duty but not something one enjoys doing. Many have had the wrong idea about the nature of prayer. The old, nonbiblical idea of prayer was that it is an agonizing, a begging of God, a paying of a price, a pleading, and a storming of the citadels of heaven until one receives what he or she asks for. The biblical attitude of the nature of prayer is one of calmly rejoicing, trusting, asking, seeking, or knocking (not pounding). This attitude changes prayer from a burdensome duty to a time of joyful fellowship with God.

Prayer is not a boring religious exercise or a liturgy to be practiced daily. It is a time of fellowship and of communication with the Heavenly Father. It is *talking with* God. It is not a litany to be recited but a talk with the Lord. Nor is it a hectic rushing into the presence of God when the storms of life strike us. It is not fervent yelling and beating one's breast to demand that God take some appropriate action (that one has decided upon) and that He take it immediately.

Instead, prayer is daily association and fellowship with God in all kinds of spiritual weather and in all the circumstances of life (good and bad). It enables people to ride through the storms of life safely.

In 1 Kings 18, the prophets of Baal prayed to their gods, and Elijah later prayed to his God. Beyond the

obvious fact that Baal was not really a god, but a fig-
ment of the imagination, one cannot help but notice
the different attitudes of the prophets of Baal and of
the lone prophet of the true God.

After the prophets of Baal had leaped on the altar,
cried aloud to Baal, and cut themselves in a vain attempt to gain the attention of their god, Elijah quietly
prayed this simple prayer: "Lord God of Abraham,
Isaac, and of Israel, let it be known this day that thou
art God in Israel, and that I am thy servant, and that I
have done all these things at thy word" (1 Kings 18:36).
There was no agonizing, no pleading, no storming the
citadels of heaven in Elijah's prayer. It was a quiet,
trustful request to the one true God.

Recall the prayer of Jesus at the tomb of Lazarus.
"Father, I thank thee that thou hast heard me. And I
knew that thou hearest me always; but because of the
people which stand by I said it" (John 11:42). Do you see
any agonizing or pleading in that prayer of Jesus? Do
you detect any note of begging or demanding?

But one might ask, "Didn't Jesus agonize in prayer
at least once in the garden of Gethsemane?" The writer
of Hebrews wrote, speaking of Jesus, "Who in the days
of his flesh, when he had offered up prayers and suppli-
cations with strong crying and tears unto him that was
able to save him from death, and was heard in that he
feared" (Heb. 5:7).

If one remembers the story, Jesus received a *no* answer to His request to be spared death. But Jesus had
also said, "Nevertheless not my will, but thine, be
done" (Luke 22:42). His prayer was answered, not because He agonized but because "He feared." Jesus re-
coiled from being outside the will of His Heavenly Father more than He agonized over the thought of death

on the cross.

This single incident of Jesus' agonizing in prayer does not teach people that they should do the same. Jesus did not receive what He agonized for. And, the fact that He didn't enables people to have forgiveness of sins. Effective praying does not need to be by strong crying and tears.

One young convert, a foreigner whose language is not always grammatically correct or his command of the English language what it should be, prayed this prayer: "Lord, here I is, down on these old bones of mine. My wife is home sick, but, if she dies, I bet you a nickel them little children of ours won't suffer."

When receiving answers to prayer, the experience of many is that instead of God giving people what they sometimes want, He gives them something better. For example, the story is told of a little girl going overseas with her mother on a ship. Standing at the rail, she accidentally dropped her favorite doll overboard. The child immediately ran to the captain and pleaded with him to turn the ship around to recover her doll. The captain refused, trying to explain that it would be impossible to rescue her doll. The little girl did not understand and was angry with the captain. When the ship reached port, the captain bought the little girl a new doll to replace the one she had dropped overboard. At first, she didn't like the new doll as much as the old one. But, in time, she learned to love it even more than she had loved the old doll.

Prayer is often like that. As it were, people drop their little dolls overboard, and then beg the captain (God) to turn the ship (the universe) around so that they might recover the thing, person, or health that they lost. He tells them that it is not possible. Sometimes they don't understand, and they are angry at God. Later, God often gives them something or some person to help replace the one they lost. Remember that when prayers seem unanswered, perhaps God has something better for you.

Also, people do not have to stay awake all night until God answers their prayers. A great Christian leader was so burdened with a problem that he could not sleep. Finally, he thought he heard the voice of God speaking to him, saying, "Go to sleep. I'll sit up the rest of the night."

Read the following Scripture on the subject of answered prayer:

> This is the confidence that we have in him, that, if we ask any thing according to his will, he heareth us:
> And if we know that he hear us, whatsoever we ask, we know that we have the petitions that we desired of him" (1 John 5:14-15).

And, since we do not always know what God's will is, we need continually to pray, "Lord, teach us to pray," and "not my will but thine be done."

Or, in the words of Colonel John Glenn, the astronaut turned senator, "There is a form of space communication which is quite clear, but which is too often neglected by modern man." That form of communication is prayer.

Daily Bible Reading

Daily Bible reading is reading a portion of Scripture from one's Bible each day, just as a person eats each and every day. Why? Just as a person's body needs food every day, one's spiritual nature needs daily spiritual food. This time of Bible reading enables a person, day by day and year after year, to become better acquainted with the Bible (and God's will) than one could ever become by merely attending Sunday School, church, and a midweek Bible study. It enables a person to seek daily the will of God for his or her life.

How can one do this? A person could follow a system of Bible readings found in various devotional magazines or books. A person could read the Bible through, reading as much as he has time for each day. A person could read the Bible through in a year's time, starting at the beginning. This can be done either by reading four chapters a day, beginning in Genesis, or by reading three chapters a day from the Old Testament and one from the New Testament.

Reading the Bible through takes discipline, determination, and persistence. A person can easily become bogged down in Leviticus or Numbers and begin to question the value of reading those books. But they are worth one's time, as a person will eventually discover. One can become bogged down in the many laws of Exodus or the "begats" in some parts of the Old Testament.

For instance, in Genesis 5, a person may wonder if there is any value in reading the chapter. But a person may discover in that long list of births, marriages, children, and deaths that there was one man who did not die. He walked with God and was taken to heaven without going through death. Nothing is said of the many others concerning "a walk with God."

The books from Genesis through Esther are predominantly historical and biographical. One can learn a tremendous amount from the study of history and biography. The study of history, for instance, can help to keep us from making the same mistakes that were previously made. Some people enjoy reading biographies. In the Old Testament you will read about Adam and Eve, Noah, Abraham, Isaac, Jacob, Joseph, Moses, Joshua, Samuel, Saul, David, Solomon, Elijah, Elisha, Deborah, Hannah, Miriam, Rachel, Leah, Isaiah, Ezekiel, Daniel—and so many more.

If a person is interested in personal or social ethics, there is a wealth of teaching in these areas throughout the Word of God. If a person likes the study of prophecy, he or she will find it in the books starting with Isaiah, continuing through the last book of the Old Testament and ending in the Book of Revelation.

Bible reading and private prayer belong together. Pray as you read. Meditate as you read. Find God's "marching orders" for your life for the day. It might be profitable to take notes while you read. A valuable practice is to mark your Bible with a red and blue pencil. Someone has said that "a well-marked Bible is the sign of a well-fed Christian."

Where can a person read? Read the Bible anywhere that you can be alone, if possible. Read it the same place where you pray. *When* can a person pray? Possibly in the morning. This will give a person teachings and thoughts for the day ahead. It will fortify a person for the events of the day. *What then* does a person do? If a person continues the practice of daily Bible reading for the rest of his or her life, each year he or she will know more of God's will. A person will grow spiritually as he feeds on the Word of God. The Holy Spirit can fill a person when he or she is filled with the Word of God.

Meditation

There is confusion over the meaning of meditation. Men and women of true faith have meditated since time immemorial. Biblical meditation is not to be linked with the Eastern philosophy-religion of Transcendental Meditation. I recommend the kind of meditation that involves a time of deep thought on what one has read in his daily Bible reading.

The mere habit of reading the Bible each day has limited value if one does not meditate on what he has read and follow this with a commitment to obeying it. A person is not merely performing a religious duty, but he is letting God speak to him. Benjamin Franklin said, "Reading makes a full man. Meditation a profound man. Discourse a clear man." So discuss what one reads with other Christians.

Devotional Books and Periodicals

To read devotional books and/or devotional periodicals along with one's Bible reading and prayer is a definite help to the spiritual life. There are many such aids to be found, especially in Christian book stores and from Christian publishers.

12
Your Relationship to a Church

What does a person think when someone asks him if he belongs to a church? Does he think of a building? An organization? A denomination? The word *church* could mean any of those terms. Sometimes people think of the church as a building. In days gone by, the church building was referred to as a meeting house where the church members came together. That edifice of brick and stone is the building but not the church.

The biblical meaning of the word *church* does not refer to a building but to a group of believers who are called out of the world to be the people of God. In the biblical sense, the church cannot burn down. Even if the building burns, the people (the church) are still alive.

At times the Bible refers to the word *church* as the universal church—a spiritual group in which all true believers are united, regardless of race, color, creed, or class.

There are literally hundreds of denominations and sects in this nation. The Christian who wants to affiliate with the *church* or some denomination faces this confusing picture. Many people simply join the church in which they were brought up. Others join a church because it is located nearby. Others join a church because it is friendly. Some join a church because it has inspiring preaching, stirring music, or a wide-awake youth program. What church or denomination should each person join?

Certainly, one's decision will be based on his or her philosophy of living. If one's philosophy includes a doctrinal statement (a summary of what one believes), he will want to join a church that teaches beliefs compatible with his.

A decision should be based on a person's strategy for living, considering one's long-term, intermediate, and short-term goals. The decision to join a church should be based on finding a community of faith where one can personally worship and serve Christ in order to glorify God. When a person makes a decision on this basis, he or she is more likely to enjoy his Christianity and, of course, his life.

One should not choose a church or denomination on the basis of economics or social status. The choice should also not be made on the basis of culture, but unfortunately it often is. One's strategy for living and goals should be a major factor in determining a person's church affiliation.

Which Church Should a Person Join?

Some say, "Join the church of one's choice." Others might reword that to say, "Join the church of God's choice." Certainly, a person should pray that the Lord will lead him or her to a church that is in accordance with God's Word. (In some denominations, people are expected to join the church in their area or parish. Other denominations allow people to join any church regardless of its location.)

Should people join the church from which they *get*

the most? Or should they join the church where they can *give* the most? The church they can help? The church where they can serve the most? The church they think needs them the most? All of this assumes that a person accepts the teachings of the Bible and is where he should worship regularly.

Some people are unable to attend church because they have to work on Sunday. A Christian will try to avoid such a conflict; however there are some types of work that are needed around the clock. Some churches have a variety of scheduled services which helps in this matter. Thus, a Christian can often find worship services or Bible studies at unusual hours. Others cannot attend church because of infirmities. They are the homebound. They must worship with the aid of radio or television and those who visit on behalf of the church or other Christian group.

Too many others attend no church, even though they are quite able to do so. Some prefer to watch a religious program on television. They cannot take the place of an active association and fellowship within a local body of believers who work together in the community.

Each person should make choosing a church or a denomination a matter of prayer. Find a church where the Bible is believed and preached. Find a church where one can serve and participate in its ministry to the community. Find a church where one's family will be spiritually fed and where they will have rich fellowship with other Christians.

How Often Should a Person Attend Church?

Nowhere in the Bible does it specifically say, "Thou shalt attend church every Sunday morning and every Sunday night," plus prayer meetings, special services, and the like. It does say this: "Not forsaking the assembling of ourselves together, as the matter of some is; but exhorting one another: and so much the more, as ye see the day approaching" (Heb. 10:25). The implication is that church attendance should increase, not decrease. The experience of many thousands of Christians is that weekly worship is not an option but a necessity.

On Sunday mornings a person should not need to decide whether or not he or she is going to church, unless there is what used to be called "providential hindrance"—sickness, emergencies, an employer who insists one must work on Sunday. The decision (to go every Sunday) should have been made once and for all in the past.

How Active Should a Person Be in His or Her Church?

There are two extremes to avoid in one's church activities. One extreme is the practice of a large number of church members, which is take no active part in church other than to attend. They accept no office, teach no Sunday School class, or serve on any committee. Yet, sometimes they are the most vocal critics of the church and its pastor. Often they give the least amount of money, too.

The other extreme is the practice of a majority of members who spend so much time serving the church that they neglect their families and community organizations. Some members have half a dozen offices in the church and exert much (sometimes too much) influence in the church.

If possible, everyone should have some "job" to do in the church. It may be as one of the leaders, as a teacher in the educational program, as a visitor, as a committee member, or a caretaker of the building and grounds, according to one's abilities, talents, and spiritual gifts. If every member of one's church were as active as oneself, what kind of a church would it be?

Every church needs volunteer workers. No pastor can or should be expected to do all the "church work." Nor should the church staff of a larger church be expected to do it all. Every church, regardless of its size, needs volunteer lay workers to carry on an effective ministry.

Should a Person Ever Leave His or Her Church?

Many people leave their churches because of dissension, because they are "mad" at the pastor or disagree with what someone in the church has decided or done. Some leave one church because the pastor forgot to visit them when he should have. They may never forgive him, though forgiveness is a basic pillar of the Bible. They never return even when a new pastor comes to the church.

Whatever the reasons, no one should do what thousands of others have done—quit going to *any* church. If a person feels that he is led by God to leave a church, he should *immediately* look for a church where he can worship in spirit and in truth. If a person is looking for a perfect church or a perfect pastor, he will look in vain. There are none. Every church has its weaknesses. Everyone should have an active relationship with some church. Pray about this choice. Discuss it with the family.

God has a place of service and worship for you.

13
Your Vocation and Avocation

Vocation

A person's life work (occupation or profession) can be a major factor in helping a person enjoy life. It can also heavily contribute to dissatisfaction and boredom. Some people enter an occupation or profession as soon as they leave school and remain in it the rest of their lives. Others may change jobs frequently or even in mid-life. Others lose their jobs after middle age, causing a severe crisis. Sometimes crises appear in families where both husband and wife are employed, and one of them is transferred to another part of the country. One or both of them do not want to move. Perhaps the greatest crisis of all is unemployment which may occur at any age in life.

One's vocation is extremely serious and will affect all of one's life. That is why Christians should understand God's intention for our work life. The apostle Paul wrote: "For even when we were with you, this we commanded you, that if any would not work, neither should he eat" (2 Thess. 3:10). We also realize that some are helpless and unable to work, but Paul is not addressing the handicapped and infirm.

The Bible certainly speaks to people's responsibility to help the poor. The main problem is how to do it without making the problem worse. Temporary handouts do not solve a long-term problem. Some poor people prefer to steal for a living, and some believe they are forced into it. The apostle Paul spoke to the issue of theft versus work. "Let him that stole steal no more: but rather let him labor, working with his hands the thing which is good, that he may have to give to him that needeth" (Eph. 4:28). Some people seem to change that verse to say, "Let him that stole, steal; no more let him labour!"

Philosophy of Life

As a person reads this book, he or she probably is employed and/or one's spouse. A person may be preparing for an occupation. A person may be dissatisfied with one's present occupation for various reasons, and one may be considering a change. What factors should a person consider in choosing an occupation or a profession? Obviously, the theme of this book answers your question, at least in a general way, even if it does not suggest an occupation or a profession.

In Chapter 3, we talked about working out one's philosophy of life. The occupation or profession one chooses should be in accordance with that philosophy of life. For instance, if a person's philosophy contains a section on "values," a choice of an occupation or profession will be determined by that value system. If a person prizes people more than things, he may feel that God is leading him to an occupation or profession where one's work reflects that.

Strategy for Living

In Chapter 4, a strategy for living was discussed. Long-range, intermediate, and short-term goals were set up. One's occupation or profession should help a person to reach those goals.

One's Job and God's Glory

The theme of this book has been that the most enjoyment in life comes to the person who lives for the glory of God. Will a person's job bring glory to God and enjoyment to him?

A man came to me when I was his pastor, asking if he should quit his job. He drove a truck for a brewery. Can that kind of a job be for the glory of God? Another man in an executive position found that he was expected to drink alcoholic beverages at the social functions of his company. Could he keep that job and glorify God? A woman quit her job as a secretary because her boss expected her to tell lies on the telephone and wanted certain sexual favors. She knew that she could not glorify God in that job.

If a person has settled into one's job, occupation, or profession and believes that he or she can do that work to the glory of God, for the good of others, and for one's own enjoyment and income, then he should do the work in a manner compatible with God's will.

Perhaps a person owns a small business. Should she refuse to hire people who are not "born-again" Christians? Or should she actively promote religion on the job? Perhaps one man fires anyone who does anything contrary to his moral ideas. Do you think this man's policy is right? Another man gives preference to Christians when he is hiring. He does not "harass" his employees or try to to interfere in their private lives. He treats them fairly, pays them well, and runs his business in a way that glorifies God. Which of these two men is more likely to be a good witness for the Lord?

If a person is in college preparing for a profession but does not know what profession to choose, he can use the services of a vocational counselor, possibly a Christian counselor. A person should choose wisely the way he or she earns a living. Be sure it can be used to glorify God.

Avocation

Webster defines *avocation* as a subordinate occupation pursued in addition to one's vocation especially for enjoyment. It suggests that the word *hobby* could be a synonym for the word *avocation.* So there is little if any difference between an avocation and a hobby.

Many people receive a lot of enjoyment in life from their avocation or hobbies. This is especially true if they are not completely happy in their daily work. Some have neither an avocation nor a hobby, and they have not felt the need for one—or they could not find a suitable or enjoyable one.

One's avocation or hobby should be in agreement with his or her philosophy of life, strategy for living, and value system that is related to living for the glory of God. This way one's avocation will help bring the greatest enjoyment.

For example, being a part-time bartender on weekends would be inconsistent with a Christian's beliefs, expressed in one's philosophy of life. However, serving as a church organist would be consistent and might bring glory to God. Being a volunteer in a local hospital on one's day off could be an excellent avocation. Playing on a softball team that plays its games on Sunday mornings would be inconsistent with Christian beliefs because of the necessity for public worship every Sunday.

Being a volunteer fire fighter or working with a rescue squad could be an excellent avocation which is fully consistent with one's Christian philosophy and strategy for living. Teaching illiterate adults to read would be an excellent avocation, and it could be a means of Christian witness. Writing letters to missionaries, visiting in a nursing home, teaching a Sunday School class, or writing letters to prisoners could be consistent with one's outlook on life and would be another opportunity for Christian witness.

Engaging in various physical activities, various forms of sports, or other exercises could be helpful to a person physically, probably prolonging one's life and enabling him or her to live long enough and well enough to reach the goals he or she set for one's life. Such physical activities should be done under the guidance of your family doctor.

Avocations and hobbies that are pursued during one's working years can become one's vocation (at least part-time) after a person retires. I pursued a part-time writing ministry for many years. Now that I am retired, I write full-time.

Determined By One's Abilities, Talents, and Gifts

In Chapter 7, discovering one's abilities, talents, and gifts given by the Holy Spirit was discussed. One's choice of an avocation or hobby should be consistent with abilities, talents, and gifts.

While I was a pastor, I had two avocations—writing and church music. Pursuing musical interests in one's spare time is consistent with some inborn musical talent and an additional gift of God.

Use One's Avocation for the Glory of God

When a person finds ways to use his avocation or hobby to the glory of God, he will receive enjoyment from it that he might not have experienced had it been only a diversion for relaxation. Relaxation is good, but when it can be used for God's glory, as well as for one's health, there can be far greater enjoyment.

Try it.

14
Music in Your Life

Music is key in many people's lives, whether or not one enjoys it. If people listen to the radio, watch television, or walk through a shopping mall, they will hear music—sometimes too loud, sometimes softer. Some people may not have any interest in music. At a public event, when the national anthem is sung, some may simply stand there. Many may not participate because they are tone deaf, think they sound bad, or are petrified of letting people hear them.

Most people have some interest in music. At church they join in the singing of the hymns. At a sporting event they may sing the national anthem. Some sing and/or play an instrument. Music brings tremendous enjoyment into their lives. They may become professional musicians, but most of them will remain amateurs who play or sing only for their own enjoyment.

Music has a long and interesting history—both sacred and secular music. Music can be used as a therapeutic agent for the physically or mentally ill person. Music can excite or calm, inspire or degrade. It can be used of God or by Satan.

Being consistent with the theme of this book, the music one listens to and the music one plays or sings should be consistent with one's approach to life. Not all music brings glory to God, and not all music inspires the listener for good.

Secular Music

Some claim that music cannot be separated into the categories of secular and sacred. For them music is neutral. They may be right. Yet, for the purposes of this book, secular music will be defined as any music that has no religious words in it or is not used by the church. This is not to say that secular music has no place in the church that is determined by its suitability in the church. Musicians often divide secular music into two classifications—art music and popular or folk music.

Art music is usually what is known as "classical music." It is enjoyed by some people. One usually learns to like it. If one is reared in a home where classical music is played and loved, he usually learns to like it. Classical composers would include people such as Bach, Beethoven, Brahms, Chopin, Haydn, Mendelssohn, Mozart, Schubert, Tchaikovsky, Wagner, and others. Some of these were devout Christians, such as Johann Sebastian Bach. Bach wrote music for the glory of God. If a person enjoys classical music, he or she can enjoy many hours of pleasure listening to a record collection or attending concerts.

Popular/folk music is often thought of as the music of the people. Many folks enjoy some form of pop music. Sometimes it is easier to listen to, easier to enjoy, and easier to learn. It is heard on more radio stations than art music.

There are many kinds of popular music such as jazz, country, rock and roll, and even reggae. Many Christians believe that certain music cannot be listened to or played to glorify God, especially because of its lyrics, its beat, and how it is presented. A person can refer to the following books and magazines to find out more information about music:

Curtis, Carl, and Huff, Deborah. *Rock Music: The Cadence of Decadence?* From the *Fundamentalist Journal*, February 1986.

Johnson, Elwood Jay. *What Is Rock?* Minneapolis, Minnesota: Schmitt Hall and McCreary, 1971.

Larson, Bob. *Hippies-Hindus and Rock and Roll.* McCook, Nebraska: Bob Larson, 1969.

Larson, Bob. *Rock and Roll: The Devil's Diversion.* McCook, Nebraska: Bob Larson, 1970.

Mahoney-Schwamb, Sharon. *The Beat Goes On...But Should It?* From *The Christian Herald*, June 1985.

Peters, Dan, and Peters, Steve. *Why Knock Rock?* Minneapolis: Bethany House, 1984.

Sacred Music

Sacred music is designed to be used in church or in other religious gatherings. It may or may not have words. Just as secular music can be divided into art and pop music, so can sacred music. Some sacred music is art or classical. For instance, there are oratorios, sacred cantatas, passions, requiems, masses, and the anthems sung by many church choirs.

Hymns, Gospel Songs, and Choruses

Some familiar sacred music would include hymns, gospel songs, choruses, and a host of music often performed and heard on records. Much of this music is sung by popular gospel singers and sounds very much like secular pop music, but with Christian words.

The difference between a hymn and a gospel song is

usually determined by one fact. The gospel song has stanzas (sometimes called verses) and a chorus (or refrain). The hymn has no chorus. Usually, the hymn is more stately, more majestic, and more objective. The gospel song is usually more syncopated in rhythm and more subjective in its lyrics. "Amazing Grace" is an example of a hymn. "Since Jesus Came into My Heart" is an example of a gospel song.

The Bible on Music

A full treatment of this subject would be a book in itself. We shall only mention that the Bible has plenty of music in both the Old and New Testaments. Much music has been set to the various psalms of David and other Hebrew musicians.

A key New Testament verse on the subject of music is found in Paul's letter to the Ephesians: "Speaking to yourselves in psalms and hymns and spiritual songs, singing and making melody in your heart to the Lord" (Eph. 5:19). The last book of the Bible speaks of music being in heaven. See Revelation 4—5.

Music can lift, inspire, encourage, soothe, and draw people to a closer fellowship with God and Christian brothers and sisters. Music is one of the fine arts, along with painting, architecture, and literature.

Make a joyful noise unto the Lord!

15
Your Reading

The following information presupposes that a person can read reasonably well. I have discovered that many children unfortunately are not learning to read well in school. As adults, they may not want to read and even may not be able to read. What a handicap! Perhaps schools need to reevaluate their methods of teaching reading and their passing from one grade to the next when children have not mastered the basic skills of reading which are so necessary in today's world.

In spite of radio and television, thousands of books and magazines are published and read every year. Many people still like to read or prefer to read.

Francis Bacon in his *Essays* talks about the subject of reading in "Of Studies." Some of Bacon's words are as follows:

> Studies serve for delight, for ornament, and for ability.
>
> To spend too much time in studies is sloth, to use them too much for ornament is affectation; to make judgment wholly by their rules is the humor of a scholar.
>
> Crafty men condemn studies, simple men admire them, and wise men use them.

Concerning books, he wrote, "Some books are to be
tasted, others to be swallowed, and some few to be
chewed and digested; that is, some books are to be read
only in parts; others to be read, but not curiously; and
some read wholly, and with diligence and attention."
Bacon valued reading. He further opined, "Reading
maketh a full man, conference a ready man, and writing an exact man."

In the Bible, the Book of Ecclesiastes shows the futili-
ty and vanity (emptiness) of life apart from God. We
discover these words: "Of making many books there is
no end; and much study is weariness of the flesh" (Eccl.
12:12).

As in every other area of people's lives, the time they
spend reading and what they read should be determined by their slant on life.

Fiction

Some people have taught that reading fiction, novels, and short stories is a waste of time. This is not necessarily true. Fiction can be used by Christian writers
to teach truth to people who will not understand it in
another way. This can be true even of fiction not written by Christians. The reading of some fiction can be
both enjoyable and inspiring.

There are several kinds of fiction. There are, for instance, romantic novels, science fiction, gothic novels,
westerns, and others. Novels are written in various
lengths. Collections of short stories are also available.

One might read books listed on the best-seller lists
found in newspapers and some magazines. There are
several problems with this. One can only wonder about
the accuracy of some lists. They seldom include religious books which sometimes outsell nonreligious

books. They, of course, are not necessarily the best books but the best-sellers. Popularity does not always imply evidence of quality.

Hardly anyone can argue that books are expensive. However, the cost of books, like most everything else, has risen considerably over the years. It still remains that uplifting, entertaining, inspirational books are inexpensive in the long run because they can be read and reread and passed on to others. Some readers belong to book clubs which sell books at a discount. Besides the various secular book clubs, there are Christian book clubs (including the Broadman Readers Plan) that sell only religious books. Also, both fiction and nonfiction books can be bought on sale from various clearing houses and book stores. There is a trend in certain stores to discount all the books in stock.

Nonfiction

There are countless types of nonfiction such as "how-to" books, inspirational books, religious books, books on popular psychology, self-help books, textbooks, scholarly books, and many others. Libraries usually classify them either by the Dewey Decimal system or the Library of Congress classification. A person can find information by using either card catalogs or microcomputers (microfiche).

If a person purchases his or her own books, he might consider marking in them. Many books a person will want to reread later. One will see the advantage of having marked them.

Christian books are advertised in Christian periodicals, and ordering by mail is sometimes convenient. However, a person can look through the book before it is ordered. There is value in looking at it in a book store

first. Look at the title, author, publisher, and at least
the table of contents.

Pornography

Just as there are x-rated movies, there are x-rated
books and magazines. Some stores will not sell pornographic books or magazines. Others will sell anything
they can make a profit on. *The Christian should pa-
tronize only book stores not selling pornographic
publications.*

Reading pornography is addictive. It lowers moral
standards, and it can't be read to glorify God. Pornography cheapens human beings, making them sex ob-
jects and glorifying illicit sex. Why read pornography
when good reading material is available? When a person brings glory to God, he will enjoy Him and live to
the fullest.

The Book

An underlying principle of this book is: the greatest
reading of all is God's Holy Word. "Thy word is a lamp
unto my feet, and a light unto my path" (Ps. 119:105). It
is God's love story for all mankind. It should have precedence on all other books put together.

As Sir Walter Scott, the Scottish novelist, lay dying,
he called to his servant, "Bring me the Book," to which
the servant replied, "What book, Sir?"

Sir Walter came back with: "There is only one book,
Sir. THE BOOK—God's Holy Word!"

16
The Media

As in every other area of people's lives, what they watch, what they read, and how much time they spend doing them should be determined by their overall view of life.

Determined by Content

Any thinking Christian will agree that what people watch on TV should be determined by the content of the program. But, often, unless one has carefully read the newspapers and TV guides, they do not know the content of the program—and maybe not even then. Today, programs that were not permitted on TV in earlier years are now blatantly telecast for all to see and hear. Strong sexual content, bedroom scenes, near nudity or worse, profanity, and violence constitute a large portion of today's TV programming.

Parents and guardians need to be careful what they permit children to watch, as well as what those adults watch. TV has more influence on people (often subtly) than they realize. At first, people are shocked by the content of certain programs, but after watching them over a long period of time become insulated from the evil. People are now used to seeing what once shocked them earlier. People need to monitor carefully the amount of time that they spend watching TV. Some people watch it on an average of seven hours a day. Others may watch it all day.

Perhaps people should ask themselves these questions: (1) Is watching TV keeping me from attaining the goals I have set forth in my strategy for living? (2) Is TV keeping me from attending or being active in my church? (3) Has TV become a baby-sitting machine? (4) Am I becoming hardened and calloused to the sinful life-styles shown on many TV programs? (5) Is TV adversely affecting my health as I spend hours sitting to watch it? (6) Is TV keeping the family from any other kind of fellowship? (7) Is my whole life or my daily time schedule determined completely by TV programs?

Determined By Advertising

If a person likes sports but is opposed to people drinking alcoholic beverages, he or she is in a dilemma. A person may be annoyed by all the beer commercials televised during sports events. However, not watching the games may not keep the commercials off the screen.

Advertisers exert some influence on program content, and if people are opposed to certain programs or advertising gimmicks, they can do two things: (1) turn to another channel and (2) write to the advertiser(s) expressing their disapproval. Broadcasters do pay attention to letters and calls from viewers.

The content of some advertising is in the eyes of some Christians almost as deplorable as the TV programs themselves. People can express their disapproval by not purchasing the products of the advertisers that they object to. They can purchase the products of those whose advertising is in good taste.

Evaluation of Some TV Programs

Children's Shows. Some programs are healthy and wholesome, others acceptable, and some too violent and/or too suggestive. Watching certain kinds of programs featuring horror and violence can cause children—and sometimes even adults!—to have nightmares. Monitor what the family watches.

Soap Operas. They are addictive. The life-style of the characters is far below biblical standards. Adultery is glossed over by calling it "an affair," "a meaningful relationship," or even more revolting terms.

Situation Comedies. They are amusing. However, some of them portray people whose life-styles are definitely not within biblical bounds. They often portray the secular humanist life-style—God is out or either ridiculed.

Movies. An entire book would be essential here. Like all else in the media, there are the good, the bad, and the ugly—also the indifferent. The rating system is a farce. Many a family-type plot is tainted by random curse words—even the taking of God's name in vain—to insure that a motion picture will be rated PG or R. Many Christians have virtually quit going to the movie houses due to the constant surprises in language and behavior, even in so-called PG-rated movies. I am not suggesting that you never attend a movie, though many have already made that decision, but I am suggesting that you be careful for the sake of your testimony and your family.

Sports. These events dominate the networks, especially on weekends. About all that takes precedence over a game is an extremely important news item, like the San Francisco earthquake of October 1989 which occurred just as a World Series game was about to begin between San Francisco and Oakland, and millions actually watched the effects of the quake on their television sets.

News. Some people are loud in their protests against any censorship of news telecasts, but every news telecast actually censors out what it wants to. The very choice of what producers put in their telecasts could be called a form of censorship. Do you remember the state dignitary in the East who committed suicide on live television? Some stations later televised the actual self-shooting, whereas others did not show the shooting but rather edited out that "moment of truth." Biases in the media are often blatant.

Looking at all of these TV programs, one of the subtle yet unfair practices of the TV networks is how they treat, neglect, or portray religion (of all faiths) and the clergy. They also seldom ever show people going to church or the synagogue. The characters on many TV programs live as if there were no God and no church, except for when there are weddings and funerals. Christians are usually portrayed, if they are shown at all, as fanatics, stupid idiots, or hypocrites. Likewise, most clergy on TV are portrayed as hypocritical, stupid, intolerant, fanatical, and/or plain obnoxious. This is an unfair and untrue picture of most clergy. The public begins to assume that all preachers and churches are two-faced money-grabbers and that no clergyman or religious body is worthy of trust. Of course, all of these public scandals have led many to stereotype ministers and churches.

As in all of society, many writers and producers of movies and TV programs are not themselves interested in the church, Christianity, or any other religion.

These TV executives are often prejudiced against religious values and ideals. Some have publicly called themselves humanists. Instead of a Christ-centered life, humanism teaches that life should be man-centered. "If it feels good, then do it" is often the prevailing philosophy.

Newspapers

Newspapers have some advantages over television though they have disadvantages, too. One can be selective in what one reads in a newspaper. On television one usually watches the entire program, and at times it can be intended to entertain more than to inform. Newspapers normally carry less offensive content than television, except for certain tabloids or for dailies that major in "yellow journalism." A person can read newspapers at his convenience. However, TV news must be watched when it is aired. One old radio show had a motto which has stuck with this writer. "The freedom of the press is a flaming sword. Hold it high. Guard it well."

Radio

When television proliferated in the late 1940's and early 1950's many thought it was bye-bye to radio. According to the FCC, there are far more radio stations today than ever before. In a number of cities across the nation, there has emerged the station which specializes in "shock radio" with programming that is obscene, vulgar, gross—yes, and downright vile. Because of effective protests, though, many of these stations have had to alter their programming or go out of business.

There are many advantages to radio, the first of which is: you don't have to look—you just have to listen. You can drive your car or work around the house or in the yard. There is infinite variety. Even in some small towns, there are several stations which feature news, special events, music, and the like. Even with radio, the listener must exercise wise discretion. Some of the most detrimental music around can be found on some radio stations.

So, you are called on to discipline yourself in what you see, hear, and dwell on in your mind. It makes a difference.

17
Life-style Evangelism

It is apparent from the Bible that evangelism is the mission of the church and its members. Jesus delivered His Great Commission to the church in these words: "Go ye, therefore, and teach all nations, baptizing them in the name of the Father, and of the Son, and of the Holy Ghost: Teaching them to observe all things whatsoever I have commanded you" (Matt. 28:19-20).

Since this book is addressed to individuals rather than to the church as a body of believers, evangelism will be addressed to individual Christians, which is called personal evangelism, witnessing, or sharing one's faith—life-style evangelism. Few people seem to engage in this practice, which is taught by the Bible. Many simply do not know how to do it. Many others are afraid or are too shy to do it. Still others feel that urging people to accept Jesus as Lord and Savior is an invasion of their privacy.

Each Christian should set some time apart for sharing their faith with others. It not only glorifies God but is a source of enjoyment, not a burdensome duty.

Determined by One's Abilities, Talents, and Gifts

Everyone can not be as effective and successful as some others in the area of Christian witness, just as all cannot be preachers. Some have a definite gift for personal evangelism, a talent for sharing their faith, and the ability to witness without fear or timidity. Others definitely do not.

Sometimes people attend church where they hear a sermon on the need for sharing their faith with others. They leave feeling guilty because they do not do it or (they feel) cannot do it. If God has not given a person the gift of evangelism, He no doubt has given him or her the ability to witness to others in some way or another.

Public Evangelism

Evangelism may be divided into two categories: public (such as preaching the gospel) and personal (individual sharing of one's faith). Public evangelism is done in worship services or in special weeks of evangelism or revival.

Public evangelism, the holding of evangelistic services and revivals, was once much more effective than it seems to be today. There was a time when it was easier to reach people through evangelistic services. It is difficult today. There is the competition of TV, working wives, children with homework to do, automobiles that carry people elsewhere, and the fact that many regard public evangelism as fanatical. Possibly the days of public evangelism are waning. Let us hope not, because public evangelism has brought millions into the kingdom of God.

All of us, I am sure, are sick about hearing the foibles of certain evangelists. Simply because there are a few disappointments does not mean all evangelists are in the same boat. It is hoped that public evangelism will not be either disgraced or proven ineffective. Yet, it sometimes appears that the times in which we live are not conducive to public evangelism in the local church.

Personal Evangelism

Personal evangelism is sharing of one's faith one-on-one. When an average church advertises that it will conduct classes in personal evangelism and witnessing, the response will usually be quite meager. All too often we spent time studying evangelism and soul-winning but never do anything about it. There are all kinds of avenues for witnessing. Christians can place tracts under the windshield wipers of cars in parking lots. Most people, however, will not read the tracts and will litter the parking lot with them. As a young man, I once stopped to talk to an on-duty traffic policeman about his soul. That probably was an inappropriate time and place for personal witnessing.

However, more people refrain from witnessing at all than doing inappropriate witnessing because of their fear of ridicule and their shyness about the matter. And there are many today who claim people have no right to "inflict" religion on others. They argue that religion is a private matter. If that were totally true, there would be no church today.

There must be "a more excellent way" to share the faith with others, a way that produces joy in a person's life and to those to whom we witness—a way that is not a burdensome duty and is more effective than tract distribution and buttonholing strangers. That way is known as life-style evangelism.

Life-style Evangelism

Life-style evangelism does not annoy people by engaging them in unwanted conversation about religion.

It does not aggressively try to force religion "down the throats" of unwilling victims. It does not push or inflict one's religion on others.

Life-style evangelism *does* witness, first, by one's life. That is of prime importance because witnessing about Jesus Christ in one's living life does demonstrate effective evangelism. Secondly, it influences others by casual conversation with people with whom one already has a friendly relationship. For example, one shares his faith with members of the family, friends, neighbors, and fellow workers (not on company time). One first establishes a personal relationship with another person. Then and only then can one approach the other person about a relationship to God through Jesus Christ. Thus, the person who is the object of one's witness already has a good relationship with the person witnessing. Often, this type of evangelism grows out of helping people in need—the sick, the hospitalized, and those in trouble.

The Church Growth Institute in California asked 14,000 lay people what or who was responsible for their coming to Christ and to the church. Less than 10 percent credited a pastor, evangelistic services, or a visitation program. About 90 percent testified they owed their introduction to the Christian faith to a relative or friend.

This kind of evangelism may not win people to Christ in a few minutes. (Neither does any other kind.) This type of evangelism may take weeks, months, or even years. However, in the long run it is more effective than other types of evangelism because it does not alienate people. It usually does not turn them off or turn them against Christianity and the church.

Every Christian has a mandate to witness for Christ.

It is better to start and make a few mistakes than never to begin at all. Jesus declares, "Ye shall be witnesses unto me . . ." (Acts 1:8). Live your faith. Share it through your life and your lips.

18
Ready for Any Eventuality

Retirement can be the beginning of the "golden years" or the worst time of one's life. It will be determined by one's health, economic condition, and advanced planning.

In today's society, men and women are expected to retire at a certain age, usually sixty-two or sixty-five. Some people are able to retire much younger. Others never retire or are never required to retire. Presidents and justices of the Supreme Court seldom retire. They just "fade away," like General Douglas MacArthur spoke of. Some ministers do not retire until they are broken in health or are forced to retire.

When a person retires and what one does will be determined by one's philosophy of life, strategy for living, and how one wants to bring glory to God. A person's strategy for living will need updating when he or she is ready to retire.

When to Prepare for Retirement

People should begin to plan for retirement no later than their twenties. That sounds silly, but it's true. If people never plan their retirement until they retire, it may be too late. Even though I do not advocate asking about retirement as one's first question of his or her first employer, a person should begin to plan his or her retirement when one accepts his or her first job. Eventually, people should find out what their present job offers them when they reach retirement age.

If people are planning to live off Social Security when they retire, they had better plan to find an additional means of putting aside money for that "rainy day." If Social Security is still available when one retires, it probably will not be enough to live on, except at the poverty level. Also, plan what you will do with your time when retirement arrives. This decision should be made many years before you reach retirement age.

Stages in the Life of Adults

Eighteen. A person is now considered a young adult. He or she has graduated from high school. He or she is now able to vote and enter the work force.

Twenty-two. If one has gone to college, he is ready to enter the work force, unless he will proceed with graduate studies. (Many combine graduate studies with a job.)

Thirty. In the eyes of some, he or she is already "over the hill." Cheer up! The best days lie ahead.

Thirty-five. A person has probably reached the true midpoint of his or her life, assuming he or she will live to be about seventy or seventy-five. One begins to realize that life is half over, more or less.

Forty. Some people used to say, "Life begins at forty." It also is supposed to be the time of the much-discussed mid-life crisis for men and women.

Sixty-five. The age when the majority of people will retire unless they own their own business. At this age a person is considered "young and old." (*Old* old begins ten years later.)

What Does a Person Do When He or She Retires?

Nothing? If a person intends to spend his retirement doing nothing but lounging in a recliner watching the "boob tube," he will probably die young and not enjoy what life is left. Retirement ought to be a time when people stop doing what they have been doing to earn a living all of their adult life and do something else—something they've wanted to do for many years.

This writer had written hundreds of articles, devotions, and Sunday School lessons for years. Now that I am retired, I spend most of my time writing books. Others who can afford it spend their retirement traveling all over the world, seeing places they have wanted to see. Many retirees give some of their time to volunteer work, perhaps in a local hospital or nursing home because they didn't have time to do that when they were in the work force. Now that they have retired, they have the time. People are needed in such places, and there are seldom enough volunteers to meet those needs.

Other retirees further their education. Some colleges give discounts to senior citizens. Continuing education need not cease when people retire. Learning as a retiree can be a lot more enjoyable than when one was sixteen or twenty. Some retirees are active in church work. One's pastor can probably find something for a person to do for the church. Most churches could use many more volunteer workers. Some catch up on the reading they did not have time to do when they were younger.

Others prefer to spend their hours hunting and fishing or participating in some relatively active sport. Many realize that they must continue to exercise to keep fit and reasonably healthy. Check with one's physician about the best exercise.

Hopefully, people have enjoyed their entire life in spite of a few tragedies, illnesses, and problems. Retirement years can be the best years of one's life. It is up to each person.

Where Does a Person Live When Retired?

A person's financial condition will, of course, be a big factor in deciding where he or she will live. Some will move to Florida or Arizona. Others will remain in the area where they lived when they retired. Many advise others to remain where they are when they retire because of friends and familiar surroundings. The doctor one has trusted and the church where one has worshiped for many years is right there.

What About a Person's Financial and Physical Needs?

If a person can remain active, mentally and physically, retirement can be lengthened somewhat. Could one be happy in a nursing home? Could one be happy if homebound? Unable to drive? Could a person be dependent on others to take care of one's needs? What about going through a "second childhood?"

It will not be easy, but many enjoy life in spite of these handicaps. The joy (and their previous disposition) of their earlier lives carries over. They accept their disabilities and become interested in others rather than just themselves. A person can sometimes no longer go to church. However, one can spend a lot of time praying for one's pastor, family, friends, missionaries, government officials, and many others. One can

find religious services on the TV, radio, and services by
churches and groups which visit the retirement and
nursing homes.

Terminal Illness

For most people, terminal illness will not be considered a time to enjoy life, especially if there is pain and
physical or mental disability. Yet, at least to some degree, it can be a time of enjoyment to the extent that
people are prepared for it. The time to prepare for
death is when a person is in the prime of life. If people
wait until their final illness, it may be too late.

For the child of God, death is not an empty room that
one enters. Nor is it extinction. A person's body will rot
no matter how long its stays in a steel casket with a
concrete vault. For the child of God, death is the door-
way into heaven, the presence of God, and *greater enjoyment than one could ever have in this life in one's
present body*.

As was stated earlier, "The chief end of man is to glorify God and to enjoy Him forever." Therefore, facing
death means that people are about to enter into that
place and *state* where they will have *the most enjoyable
experiences* possible as the children of God.
375

In summary, retirement can be the most enjoyable
time of a person's life on earth, if it is planned for carefully and reasonable health and economic soundness
are experienced. And if retirement turns into terminal
illness, a person faces an even greater enjoyment, as he
or she realizes he or she will spend eternity with the
Triune God—Jesus the Son, the Heavenly Father, and
the blessed Holy Spirit.

It's Your Life—Enjoy It! There is nothing like living

with and for God. The dividends are eternal and never-changing. Your "cup runneth over . . . surely goodness and mercy shall follow you all the days of your life, and you will dwell in the house of the Lord forever" (see Ps. 23).

In Memoriam

Dr. Carlton Myers, the author of *It's Your Life—Enjoy It!*, enjoyed life to the fullest here . . . and now he is enjoying it up there. On October 27, 1989, as this book was being prepared for publication, the Lord called Dr. Myers home. Two days later, a memorial service was conducted at First Baptist Church, Ashland, Virginia.

His wife, Vera, shares these verses:

> And we know that all things work together for good to them that love God, to them who are the called according to his purpose (Rom. 8:28).

> I have fought a good fight, I have finished my course, I have kept the faith (2 Tim. 4:7).

> For me to live is Christ, and to die is gain (Phil. 1:21).

> Precious in the sight of the Lord is the death of his saints (Ps. 116:15).